THE ROMANS SPEAK FOR THEMSELVES BOOK I

SELECTIONS FROM LATIN LITERATURE FOR FIRST YEAR STUDENTS

by

Sara Adkins, Sara Honig, John McVey, Gilbert Lawall,
James Meyer, Michael Muchmore, Sean Smith, Susan Twitchell,
and Jean Waddell

Edited by

Gilbert Lawall

Longman
New York & London

The Romans Speak for Themselves, Book I

Longman, 95 Church Street, White Plains, N.Y. 10601

Associated companies:
Longman Group Ltd., London
Longman Cheshire Pty., Melbourne
Longman Paul Pty., Auckland
Copp Clark Pitman, Toronto
Pitman Publishing Inc., New York

Executive editor: Lyn McLean
Cover design: Charlene Felker
Cover photo: Alinari/Art Resource
Photo research: Aerin Csigay
Production supervisor: Eduardo Castillo

ISBN 0-8013-0267-6

CDEFGHIJ-ML-959493929190

Photo Credits and Sources

Page 2: Scala/Art Resource, NY. Page 5: Marburg/Art Resource, NY. Page 11: From *Two Roman Mice* by Horace, retold and illustrated by Marilynne K. Roach; Thomas Y. Crowell Company © 1975 by Marilynne K. Roach. Page 21: Ashmolean Museum. Page 23: Reprinted by permission of the publishers and The Loeb Classical Library from *Pliny: Letters and Panegyricus*, translated by Betty Radice, Cambridge, Massachusetts: Harvard University Press, 1969. Page 39: Alinari/Art Resource, NY. Page 41: The Bettmann Archive. Page 42: From *Everyday Life in Ancient Rome* by F. R. Cowell, reprinted by permission of B. T. Batsford, Ltd. Page 47: Bardo Museum, Tunis. Page 51: Staatliche Antikensammlungen und Glyptothek, Munich. Pages 67 and 69: From *City* by David Macaulay; Copyright © 1974 by David Macaulay; reprinted by permission of Houghton Mifflin Company. Page 73: The Mansell Collection. Page 79: Rheinisches Landesmuseum, Trier, Germany. Page 81: Alinari/Art Resource, NY. Page 85: Fototeca Unione, at the American Academy in Rome. Page 87: Soprintendenza ai Monumenti del Lazio, Archivio Fotografico, Monumento a Vittorio Emanuele II, Via Aracoeli, Roma. Page 91: Alinari/Art Resource, NY. Page 95: The Mansell Collection. Page 97: Reproduced by Courtesy of the Trustees of the British Museum.

CONTENTS

PREFACE FOR STUDENTS

In this book you will find fourteen passages from Latin authors chosen to accompany the cultural topics in ECCE ROMANI Books 1 and 2. All of the authors except Erasmus lived in the ancient Roman world. Each passage has been adapted so that it may be read at a designated point in the course of your learning of Latin from the ECCE ROMANI series. The passages are drawn from some of the greatest and most interesting Roman authors such as Catullus, Horace, Ovid, and Pliny and cover a wide variety of topics from the family to ghost stories and the chariot races.

We have provided a number of features that will help you in your encounter with what these Romans had to say:

1. Each chapter begins with a brief introduction, which will orient you to the topic of the Latin passage and provide some background and context for your reading of the Latin.
2. On the page opposite each segment of the passage is a vocabulary list that gives all of the words that you have not met yet in your reading in ECCE ROMANI.
3. Beneath each passage on the right-hand page you will find comprehension questions that are designed to lead you to an understanding of what the author is saying in the passage. These questions will help you comprehend and translate the Latin.
4. We then provide you with a copy of the entire passage without vocabulary but with questions that invite discussion of the passage or with suggestions of other activities that will help bring the passage alive as an actual communication from a Latin writer.

As you use this book, focus on the Latin. Listen to what the Romans had to say about themselves and about the world in which they lived. Let the Romans speak for themselves, but listen carefully to their voices. Let your reading of the following passages be an enjoyable, enriching encounter with inhabitants of a world distant from us in time and space—with people who were very different from us yet share many of our thoughts and feelings. Enjoy your encounter with them!

ACKNOWLEDGMENTS

All but two of the chapters in this book were written by graduate students in the program leading to a Master of Arts in Teaching Latin and Classical Humanities at the University of Massachusetts at Amherst; they were written as partial fulfillment of the requirements of Latin 608, Teaching Latin Literature, taught by Professor Gilbert Lawall in spring semester, 1984. These students were Sara Adkins, Sara Honig, John McVey, James Meyer, Michael Muchmore, Sean Smith, Susan Twitchell, and Jean Waddell.

The materials were revised in 1986 by Donald Benander, Latin teacher and Head of the Foreign Language Department at Chicopee High School, Chicopee, Massachusetts. Two chapters were added by Gilbert Lawall for this edition. Professor Conrad Barrett of California State University, Long Beach, and David Perry of Rye High School, Rye, New York, served as consultants in the preparation of this edition and made numerous useful suggestions that have been incorporated into the lessons.

During the spring semester, 1988, Marjorie Keeley, also a candidate in the program leading to a Master of Arts in Teaching Latin and Classical Humanities at the University of Massachusetts at Amherst, helped in many ways with preparation of the final manuscript, including compilation of the vocabulary at the end of this book. She also wrote the translations and offered many suggestions that have been included in the teacher's handbook.

The editor, Gilbert Lawall, wishes to thank all those who have contributed to this project.

1
THE FAMILY IN ROMAN SOCIETY

Catullus, Poem 61, lines 204–223

(after Chapter 2)

INTRODUCTION

Gaius Valerius Catullus was born at Verona in northern Italy. He lived from about 84 to about 54 B.C. As a youth he moved to Rome, where he made a home.

Poem 61 by Catullus is a wedding song sung by young men and girls before the bridal chamber, in honor of the marriage of Manlius Torquatus and Aurunculeia. In this passage from the poem, family life is celebrated. Man and woman are "joined together" in marriage **(coniugium)** with the hope that their marriage may prove fruitful **(fēlīx).** The wish that the marriage produce a child is the central theme of the passage. The importance of children is clearly stated: it is through offspring that the good family name **(nōmen)** will be passed along to successive generations. The comparison that follows introduces a major consideration in a Roman marriage: the character of the wife. If she is to be a suitable mother, she must first be an exemplary wife and possess what the Romans called **pudīcitia** ("chastity," "purity," "virtue"). The reputation of the wife must be flawless: she must always remain faithful to her husband. The term **ūnivira** was applied to such a woman:

> To have had a single husband was considered a feminine virtue, and the epithet **ūnivira** is one of the chief titles of honor in the sepulchral epitaphs of married women. Women who regarded conjugal loyalty lightly incurred severe disapproval. The **cōnūbium** was thus in every way a very powerful bond among the Romans, who founded their empire and their civilization on the sanctity of family life.
>
> —Paoli, *Rome: Its People, Life, and Customs,* pages 115–116

A child's future was determined in part by the virtue of his or her mother. Penelope, the wife of Ulysses, was the embodiment of the virtuous wife in ancient society. She faithfully awaited her husband's return from the Trojan War. During Ulysses' nineteen-year absence, she attended to the needs of the household and of their son

Telemachus. His rightful place in society was secured by Penelope's faithfulness to her long-absent husband.

Here is a translation of the Latin passage that you will be reading from Catullus' wedding song:

May the marriage turn out happily!
Produce children soon!
It is not right for such an ancient name (i.e., family) to be without children.
Always produce children from the same stock:
so that a tiny Torquatus,
stretching forth his tender hands from his mother's lap,
may smile sweetly at his father with half-opened lips.
May he be like Manlius, his father, and may all easily recognize him!
May the face of the tiny Torquatus reveal the chastity of his mother!
May such praise, due to his good mother, show the worth of the family line of Torquatus,
as the fame of Telemachus is outstanding,
due to his best of mothers, Penelope.

A Roman bride and bridegroom joining hands in marriage

Below you will find the passage from Catullus' poem that you will read with the help of the notes and questions on the following pages. It will help if you read the Latin aloud and then locate the Latin words from which the English words given below the passage have been derived. You may be surprised how much of the Latin you can understand simply by thinking of the meaning of the English derivatives. Locate the Latin source of the easier English words first and then of the more difficult ones. If you do not know the meaning of an English word, look it up in an English dictionary or ask your teacher.

Coniugium fēlīciter ēveniat!
Brevī tempore līberōs date!
Nōn decet nōmen tam vetus sine līberīs esse.
Semper indidem līberōs ingenerāte:
ut Torquātus parvulus,
ex gremiō mātris suae porrigēns tenerās manūs,
dulce rīdeat ad patrem sēmihiante labellō.
Sit similis Manliō, suō patrī, et facile omnēs eum nōscitent!
Ōs Torquātī parvulī pudīcitiam suae mātris indicet!
Tālis laus ab bonā mātre genus Torquātī approbet,
quālis fāma Tēlemachī est ūnica
ab optimā mātre Pēnelopā.

A. Easier

event	semi-
brevity	similar
veteran (root meaning "old")	indicate
generate	approve
maternal	fame
tender	unique
manual	optimist
paternal	

B. More Difficult

conjugal	deride
felicity	facility
temporal	laudatory
nominal	genus

What word in the Latin means "let him smile"?

What is the full name of the husband?

1 **coniugium**, marriage
fēlīciter, luckily, happily, fruitfully
ēveniat, may it turn out
2 **līberōs**, children
date, give! produce!
3 **decet**, it is fitting, proper, right
tam, so, such
vetus, old, ancient
sine, without
esse, to be
4 **semper**, always
indidem, from the same source or stock
ingenerāte, produce! create!
5 **ut**, so that
parvulus, little, tiny. The word expresses affection.
6 **gremiō**, lap
mātris suae, of his own mother
porrigēns, stretching forth
tenerās manūs, tender hands
7 **dulce**, sweetly
rīdeat, (he) may smile
ad patrem, at (his) father
sēmihiante labellō, with a half-opened lip

CATULLUS, POEM 61, LINES 204–223

I.

Coniugium fēlīciter ēveniat!
Brevī tempore līberōs date!
Nōn decet nōmen tam vetus sine līberīs esse.
Semper indidem līberōs ingenerāte:
ut Torquātus parvulus,
ex gremiō mātris suae porrigēns tenerās manūs,
dulce rīdeat ad patrem sēmihiante labellō.

Comprehension Questions

(The numbers in parentheses refer to line numbers of the passage above.)

1. What is the poet's wish for the bridal couple? (1)
2. What does he urge them to do? (2)
3. What is not fitting for the ancient family name of this married couple? (3)
4. From what source are the offspring to come? (4)
5. How is the imagined baby Torquatus described? (5)
6. Where is he imagined as being (6)
7. What two things is he imagined as doing? (6–7)

A Roman child nursed by its mother and held by its father

8 **sit**, may he be
similis, like
facile, easily
omnēs, all, everyone
eum, him
nōscitent, may (they) recognize
9 **ōs**, face, features
pudīcitiam, chastity, purity, virtue
indicet, may (it) reveal
10 **tālis**, such
laus, praise
ab bonā mātre, from, due to (his) good mother
genus, origin, family line
approbet, may (it) show the worth of
11 **quālis**, as
fāma, fame, good name, reputation
Tēlemachī, of Telemachus, the son of Odysseus (Ulysses) and Penelope
ūnica, sole, unique, outstanding
12 **optimā**, best
Pēnelopā, Penelope (the model of a virtuous wife)

II.

Sit similis Manliō, suō patrī, et facile omnēs eum nōscitent!
Ōs Torquātī parvulī pudīcitiam suae mātris indicet!
Tālis laus ab bonā mātre genus Torquātī approbet,
quālis fāma Tēlemachī est ūnica
ab optimā mātre Pēnelopā.

Comprehension Questions

8. What is the first name of Torquatus' father? (8)
9. Why will people be able to recognize the baby? (8)
10. Whose virtue will the face of the baby reveal? (9)
11. To whom is the praise mentioned in line 10 due?
12. What will that praise show the worth of? (10)
13. To whom are Torquatus and his mother compared? (11–12)
14. How is the reputation of Telemachus described? (11)
15. How is his mother described? (12)

THE PASSAGE AS A WHOLE FOR DISCUSSION

Coniugium fēlīciter ēveniat!
Brevī tempore līberōs date!
Nōn decet nōmen tam vetus sine līberīs esse.
Semper indidem līberōs ingenerāte:
ut Torquātus parvulus,
ex gremiō mātris suae porrigēns tenerās manūs,
dulce rīdeat ad patrem sēmihiante labellō.
Sit similis Manliō, suō patrī, et facile omnēs eum nōscitent!
Ōs Torquātī parvulī pudīcitiam suae mātris indicet!
Tālis laus ab bonā mātre genus Torquātī approbet,
quālis fāma Tēlemachī est ūnica
ab optimā mātre Pēnelopā.

Discussion Questions

1. The Latin word for marriage, **coniugium (con-** "with" **+ iungere** "to join") literally means "a yoking together." What does this tell us about the Romans' concept of marriage? How does it compare with ours?
2. How do the first four lines of the passage emphasize the importance of children in a Roman family? Point to specific words in your answer.
3. Basing your answer upon Catullus' portrayal of Torquatus and the illustration of members of a Roman family on page 5, how do you think the Romans felt about children?
4. Explain from the passage why it was so important to the Romans to have offspring.
5. In the last four lines who (mother, father, or child) is emphasized?
6. According to this passage, what qualities of the mother are most important?
7. Of what importance is the virtue of the mother to her son? Explain the comparison to Penelope and Telemachus.
8. Is virtue such as that of Penelope or of Torquatus' mother still valued in today's society? If so, to what extent?

Word Study

The English word *matrimony*, meaning "marriage," comes from the Latin word **mātrimōnium**. The Latin phrase **in mātrimōnium dūcere** meant litrerally "to lead into motherhood." What does this Latin expression tell us about Roman attitudes toward marriage and family?

THE ROADS OF ROMAN ITALY
0
100
Miles
Augusta Praetoria
Comum
Mediolanum
Segusio
Placentia
Cremona
Verona
Aquileia
Mantua
Dertona
Po
Genua
Ravenna
Ariminum
Luna
Florentia
Fanum Fortunae
Pisae
Arretium
Vada Volaterrana
Tiber
Truentum
ADRIATIC SEA
Reate
Aternum
Tibur
Corfinium
CORSICA
ROME
Anagnia
Fregellae
Beneventum
Capua
Canusium
Formiae
Cales
Misenum
Neapolis
Venusia
Brundisium
Tarentum
SARDINIA
TYRRHENIAN SEA
Rhegium
SICILY
1 Via Aemilia (187 B.C.)
2 Via Appia (312 - 244 B.C.)
3 Via Aurelia
4 Via Flaminia (220 B.C.)
5 Via Latina
6 Via Postumia (148 B.C.)
7 Via Valeria
8 Via Julia Augusta
9 Via Domitiana
10 Via Trajana
11 Via Cassia
12 Via Popillia
13 Via Salaria

2
ROMAN ROOTS IN THE COUNTRY

Horace, *Satires* II.6

(after Chapter 7)

INTRODUCTION

Quintus Horatius Flaccus, known to us as Horace, was born in Venusia, a town in southern Italy, in 65 B.C., and he died at the age of 57 in 8 B.C. His father was a freedman who worked as a successful auctioneer. Despite his humble birth, Horace was given an excellent education by his father; he was sent to well-known teachers in Rome and then attended the university in Athens. When civil war broke out after Julius Caesar was assassinated, he took sides with Brutus, whom he had met while attending school in Athens. After Brutus was defeated in battle in 42 B.C., Horace reconciled his differences with the victorious Octavian and received a full and honorable pardon.

Upon returning to Rome, Horace found that his father had passed away and that his property had been confiscated. He was able, however, to obtain a minor post in the treasury department of Rome, and this gave him barely enough to live on. Half jokingly, Horace tells us that at this point in his life he was driven to writing poetry because he had lost all of his property in the civil war. Horace's poetry soon caught the attention of the poet Vergil, who was to become his close friend. In 38 B.C. Vergil introduced Horace to Maecenas, the man who was responsible for collecting and promoting a small circle of elite writers under the patronage of Octavian. From this point on, Horace was able to live and move freely among the upper levels of Roman society.

Horace wrote several types of poetry, including pieces that can best be termed "conversations" **(sermōnēs)**, although they are now usually called satires. The selections given here are from one of Horace's best-known conversational sketches or satires, about a country mouse and a city mouse. What did country life mean to the Romans?

Country life represented the agrarian roots of the Roman people. Rome became great because of the character of the early Romans, who were predominantly farmers. When Horace writes about the rustic life, he is invoking in his audience a recollection of simpler and more upright times in the past. He is taking the listeners back to their ancestral roots and returning them to a time when good and evil were clearly etched in black and white. The Roman audience would have been reminded of a folk hero such as the farmer Cincinnatus, who rose to meet a crisis as a national leader when he was needed and then returned to his farm once the crisis was over. Cincinnatus was an example of what the Romans meant when they spoke about the **mōs maiōrum** ("the customs of our ancestors"). These customs, which were highly valued by the Romans, were based on virtues such as simplicity, honesty, contentment, and generosity.

Horace's audience would have easily recognized the subtle implications in his sketch about a city mouse and a country mouse. Each mouse represents a different way of life. A smooth city slicker is compared with a simple rustic. While the Romans professed a preference for the simple, unadorned life that the country mouse represents, in reality most wealthy, educated Romans in the time of Horace spent most of their time enjoying the luxury and excitement of city living and put up with the discomforts and dangers that went along with it.

There was thus a basic tension between what the Romans said and what they did. Nonetheless, Romans like Horace enjoyed thinking of themselves as a simple, agrarian people. The following tale would have reinforced that self-image.

1 **hoc**, this
vōtum, prayer
modus agrī, a measure of land
ita, so, very
2 **sit**, there may be
aquae fōns, a spring of water
fluēns, flowing
parva, small, little
super hīs, in addition to these

4 **fābula**, story
nārrat, (he, she) tells
ōlim, once (upon a time)
mūs, mouse
fertur, is said
accēpisse, to have received
5 **urbānus**, of the city, from the city
mūrem, mouse
cavus, hole, cave
pauperī, poor, humble
ambō, both
erant, (they) were
veterēs, old
6 **aspera**, rough, harsh
vīta, life
agēbat, (he, she) was leading (a life, **vītam**)
cibus, food
parcēbat, (he, she) was careful to use little (+ **cibō**)
tamen, nevertheless
7 **hospitī**, to (his) guest
artus, tight, thrifty
animus, mind, heart
aperuit, (he, she) opened

HORACE, *SATIRES* II.6

I.

Horace begins by expressing a simple wish:

Hoc est vōtum meum: modus agrī nōn ita magnus, ubi hortus sit et prope vīllam aquae fōns semper fluēns et parva silva super hīs.

Comprehension Questions

1. For what does Horace pray? (1)
2. What three features of a farm does he mention in the second line of his prayer?
3. Where is the spring to be and how is it described? (2)
4. What does Horace want in addition? (2–3)

II.

Later in the satire, Horace has his neighbor Cervius relate the fable of the country mouse and city mouse:

Cervius fābulam nārrat: "Ōlim mūs rūsticus fertur accēpisse urbānum mūrem in cavō pauperī. Ambō erant amīcī veterēs. Mūs rūsticus asperam vītam agēbat. Cibō parcēbat, sed tamen hospitī artum animum aperuit.

Comprehension Questions

5. What does Cervius do? (4)
6. What is the country mouse said to have done? (4–5)
7. Where did the country mouse entertain the city mouse? (5)
8. What had been the relationship between the two mice in the past? (5)
9. What kind of life was the country mouse leading? (6)
10. What attitude did he have toward food? (6)
11. What kind of a heart did the country mouse have? (7)

8 **cubāns**, reclining
gaudēbat, (he, she) was glad, was enjoying (**mūtātā sorte**)
mūtātā, changed, different
sorte, condition of life, fate, situation
bonus, good, prosperous
rēbus, things, circumstances
9 **convīva**, dinner guest
agēbat, (he, she) was playing (the role of)

10 **ingēns**, huge, loud
strepitus, screeching noise
valvārum, of the folding doors
ex lectīs, from the couches
utrumque, both of them
excussit, (he, she, it) knocked . . . from
11 **ubi**, when
domus, building, mansion, palace
alta, high, lofty
Molossōrum canum, of dogs from Molossia (a region of Greece famous for its hunting dogs)
lātrātū, barking
personuit, (it) resounded, rang with (**lātrātū**)
12 **pavidus**, trembling, frightened
triclīnium, dining room
cucurrērunt, (they) ran
tum, then
haud, not at all
mihi, me
13 **haec**, this
placet, (it) is pleasing (to) (**mihi**)
Valē! Farewell! Goodbye!
cavus, hole, cave
-que, and
tūtus, safe
ab īnsidiīs, from ambush
14 **mē**, me
sōlābuntur, (they) will console, comfort
cibō simplicī, with simple food

III.

The city mouse is shocked by the harsh conditions in which his friend is living, and he convinces the country mouse to return to the city with him. He assures the country mouse that they will have everything they want. The country mouse agrees. We pick up Cervius' narrative at the point where the city mouse is treating the country mouse to a fabulous dinner **(cēna).**

"Mūs rūsticus cubāns gaudēbat mūtātā sorte et in bonīs rēbus laetum convīvam agēbat.

Comprehension Questions

12. How is the country mouse situated? (8)
13. In what is he rejoicing? (8)
14. How are the new circumstances referred to? (8)
15. How is the country mouse behaving, or what role is he playing? (9)

IV.

A sudden intrusion makes the country mouse see city life for what it really is and makes him prefer his life in the country.

"Subitō ingēns strepitus valvārum ex lectīs utrumque excussit. Ubi domus alta Molossōrum canum lātrātū personuit, mūrēs pavidī ex triclīniō cucurrērunt. Tum mūs rūsticus, 'Haud mihi haec vīta placet!' inquit. 'Valē! Mea silva cavusque tūtus ab īnsidiīs mē sōlābuntur cibō simplicī.'"

Comprehension Questions

16. What produced a screeching noise? (10)
17. How did the two mice react to the noise? (10)
18. With what did the lofty palace echo? (11)
19. How did this affect the mice and what did they do? (12)
20. What did the country mouse say? (12–13)
21. What quality does the country mouse now appreciate about his forest and cave? (13–14)
22. In what has the country mouse now learned to find comfort? (14)

THE PASSAGE AS A WHOLE FOR DISCUSSION

I.

Hoc est vōtum meum: modus agrī nōn ita magnus, ubi hortus sit et prope vīllam aquae fōns semper fluēns et parva silva super hīs.

II.

Cervius fābulam nārrat: "Ōlim mūs rūsticus fertur accēpisse urbānum mūrem in cavō pauperī. Ambō erant amīcī veterēs. Mūs rūsticus asperam vītam agēbat. Cibō parcēbat, sed tamen hospitī artum animum aperuit.

III.

"Mūs rūsticus cubāns gaudēbat mūtātā sorte et in bonīs rēbus laetum convīvam agēbat.

IV.

"Subitō ingēns strepitus valvārum ex lectīs utrumque excussit. Ubi domus alta Molossōrum canum lātrātū personuit, mūrēs pavidī ex triclīniō cucurrērunt. Tum mūs rūsticus, 'Haud mihi haec vīta placet!' inquit. 'Valē! Mea silva cavusque tūtus ab īnsidiīs mē sōlābuntur cibō simplicī.'"

Discussion Questions

1. What things are of importance to Horace on his imaginary farm? Why do you think these things in particular are of importance to him? (I)
2. How is the country mouse's life described? Are there disadvantages to country living? How is the country mouse's character portrayed? How does his character parallel his environment? (II)
3. How does the picture of life in the city (III) contrast with the previous picture of life in the country?
4. How does living in the city finally contrast with living in the country? What seems to be the main advantage of life in the country? (IV) Is there a similar tension between the attractions of city and country life within our society today?

AESOP'S FABLE

What different twist does Aesop give to the moral of the story?

Once upon a time a Country Mouse invited his friend the City Mouse for a visit. The Country Mouse lived quite a plain life, but when his guest arrived from the city, he was most hospitable and generous to his old friend, and brought out all his savings of nuts, cheese parings, bread, and barley. He knew the City Mouse was used to fancier food, but he hoped that among all his store there would be something to please. The City Mouse ate a nibble here and a nibble there, and finally said: "My dear fellow, this is all very healthy and good, no doubt, but really, you are wasting your life in this hole. A mouse lives only once, you know, and if you don't see the gay life and eat the fine food of the city now, you may never get another chance. Why don't you come to town with me, and I'll give you a taste of real life?" The Country Mouse was tempted, and they set off for town. Late at night they arrived at the great house where the City Mouse was living. The Country Mouse was shown all the fine furnishings, the silks and velvets, and then he was escorted to the dining room. There on the table were the remains of a banquet, and the City Mouse made his country cousin taste all the fine foods, and even the wine that was in the bottom of the glasses. The Country Mouse was very excited by all this grandeur, and he had made up his mind to stay, when there was a burst of noise, and the people of the house rushed in from some late party. The frightened mice scurried off the table and behind a drapery, but two dogs that had come in with the people barked at them there, and they had to run for the cellar. There the frightened little Country Mouse whispered goodbye to his friend and said: "Better to live on barley and be your own master than to live on cream at the mercy of kings."

—Translated by Thomas Bewick

3
PLINY'S LAURENTINE VILLA

PLINY, *Letters* II.17

(with "The Roman Villa," Book 1, pages 35–38)

INTRODUCTION

The Romans distinguished between two types of country homes. The **vīlla rūstica** was basically a large farm building serving many functions. There were the usual living quarters for the owner and his family and slaves, containing bedrooms, dining room, kitchen, baths, and other rooms found in a comfortable villa. In addition there were rooms for farm purposes such as stabling the animals, pressing and storing the wine, and threshing the grain. All of these were contained within one quite spacious building. The grounds around the **vīlla rūstica** grew crops, allowing the home to be self-sufficient.

The **vīlla urbāna**, on the other hand, served a very different function for its owner. This large, commodious, and luxurious building was mainly a retreat for the harried citizen who lived in the city of Rome. Always surrounded by an estate, the **vīlla urbāna** revealed the Romans' love for the beauty of the countryside. In the complexity and richness of its rooms, the **vīlla urbāna** reflected the tastes of its owner and indicated how wealthy he was. Its main function and charm were one: comfort.

The **vīlla** described in the following extract from a letter of Pliny is classified as a **vīlla urbāna**. It served as Pliny's winter residence as well as a pleasant and luxurious retreat for Pliny from the hustle and bustle of city life in Rome. The **vīlla** was located on the shore a little north of Laurentum, and so it is commonly known as the Laurentine villa.

Pliny begins his letter by describing how to get to the **vīlla** from Rome:

> You may wonder why I so enjoy my Laurentine place, but you will stop wondering as soon as you see the attractions of the house, the advantage of its location, and the extensive seafront. It is only seventeen miles from Rome, so that you can return there conveniently after completing a day's work. There is not just one way to reach it. The roads to both Laurentum and Ostia lead in that direction, but you must leave the road to Laurentum at the fourteenth milepost and the road to Ostia at the eleventh milepost. Whichever way you go, the side road is sandy and thus slow-going by cart, but easily covered on horseback. The view on either side is

full of variety. Sometimes the road narrows as it passes through the woods, but then it broadens and extends over wide meadows, where many flocks of sheep and horses and cattle are driven down from the mountains in the winter to grow sleek on the pastures in the warm spring.

Discussion Questions

1. What things would immediately impress a visitor to the **vīlla**?
2. Why is the nearness of the **vīlla** to Rome a definite advantage to Pliny?
3. Describe each of the two routes to the **vīlla** and locate the routes on the map.
4. In the closing lines of the paragraph Pliny describes, with obvious pleasure, the scenery along the road. What does this description tell you about Pliny and his values?

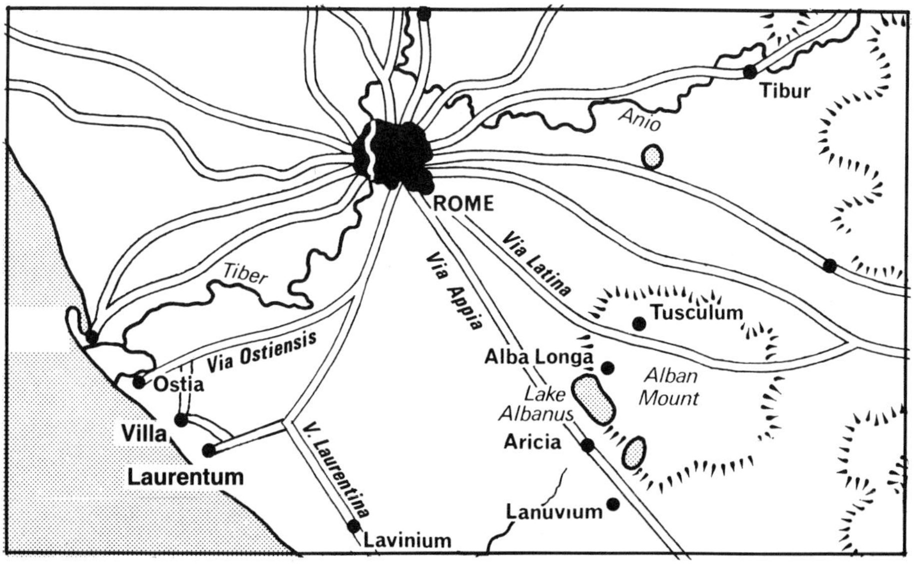

In the following parts of the letter Pliny gives an enthusiastic description of the delights of the **vīlla**. The design of the house and its location reflect Pliny's interest in having the house fit in completely with the beautiful countryside. He tells of different rooms overlooking the sea, garden suites that receive the sun at all hours of the day, and even baths from which one could look out to sea. It seems that no matter where you stood in the **vīlla** you had a beautiful view of the sea or of the surrounding countryside.

In the following passage, Pliny is describing the central axis of the **vīlla** from the entrance hall on the east through to the great **triclīnium**, which projects toward the sea on the west.

1 **ūsibus**, for use, convenience
capāx, roomy, spacious
tūtēla, upkeep, maintenance
sūmptuōsus, expensive
2 **prīmus**, first
ātrium, atrium, entrance hall, main room
frūgī, thrifty, plain
nec tamen, but not
sordidus, shabby, miserly
deinde, then, next
3 **porticūs**, colonnades, porticos, covered porches supported by columns
in . . . similitūdinem, in the likeness of
circumāctus, drawn around, rounded, curved
ārea, space, courtyard
4 **parvus**, small
fēstīvus, cheerful
inclūdunt, (they) enclose
hae, these
adversus tempestātēs, against the weather
5 **receptāculum**, shelter, refuge, retreat
ēgregius, splendid, excellent
fenestra, window
multō magis, much more
6 **tēcta**, roofs
imminentia, overhanging
eās, them (i.e., the porticos)
mūniunt, (they) protect

PLINY, *LETTERS* II.17

I.

Vīlla est ūsibus capāx, sed tūtēla nōn est sūmptuōsa. Est in prīmā parte vīllae ātrium frūgī nec tamen sordidum, deinde sunt porticūs in D litterae similitūdinem circumāctae, quae āream parvam sed fēstīvam inclūdunt. Hae porticūs sunt adversus tempestātēs receptāculum ēgregium; fenestrae et multō magis tēcta imminentia eās mūniunt.

Comprehension Questions

1. How big is the house? (1)
2. Is it expensive to keep up? (1)
3. What is the first room one would enter? (1–2)
4. What is the second area one would enter? (2–3)
5. What is the shape of the colonnades? (3)
6. What Latin words describe the area surrounded by these colonnades? (4)
7. What purpose do these colonnades serve? (4–5)
8. What protects the colonnades? (5–6)

Model of Pliny's Laurentine villa

7 **contrā mediās porticūs**, facing the middle of the porticos
cavaedium, inner hall
hilare, cheerful
mox, next
8 **triclīnium**, dining room
satis, enough, quite
pulchrum, beautiful, pretty
quod, which, that
in lītus, onto the shore
excurrit, (he, she, it) runs out, extends out
ac, and
si quandō, if ever, whenever
9 **Āfricus ventus**, African wind (i.e., the wind coming from the southwest)
mare, sea
impellit, (he, she, it) drives, stirs
frāctī, broken
flūctūs, waves
leviter, lightly, gently
10 **lavant**, (they) wash
undique, from all sides, all around
valvās, folding doors
aut, or
fenestra, window
nōn minōrēs valvīs, no smaller than the folding doors
11 **habet**, (he, she, it) has
atque, and
ita, thus
ab lateribus, from (its) sides
ab fronte, from (its) front
quasi, as if, so to speak
tria maria, three seas
12 **prospectat**, (he, she, it) looks out on, faces toward
ab tergō, from (its) back, rear
respicit, (he, she, it) looks back on
porticum, colonnade, portico, covered porch supported by columns
13 **rūrsus**, again
longinquus, far away
montēs, mountains

A. Entrance hall (**ātrium**)
B. Courtyard (**ārea**) surrounded by porticos (**porticūs**)
C. Inner hall (**cavaedium**)
D. Dining room (**triclīnium**)
E. Bedroom
F. Bedroom
G. Gymnasium
H. Bedroom
I. Bedroom
J. Slaves' rooms
K. Bedroom
L. Small dining room
M. Rooms and antechambers
N. Bathrooms
O. Heated swimming-bath
P. Ball court
Q. Suite with upper story
R. Dining room, with storage rooms above
S. Garden with vine pergola
T. Rooms behind dining room
U. Kitchen garden
V. Covered arcade
W. Terrace
X. Pliny's private suite
Y–Z. Kitchens and storerooms

II.

Est contrā mediās porticūs cavaedium hilare, mox est triclīnium satis pulchrum, quod in lītus excurrit; ac sī quandō Āfricus ventus mare impellit, triclīnium frāctī flūctūs leviter lavant. Undique triclīnium valvās aut fenestrās nōn minōrēs valvīs habet atque ita ab lateribus et ab fronte quasi tria maria prospectat; ab tergō respicit cavaedium, porticum, āream, porticum rūrsus, mox ātrium, silvās et longinquōs montēs.

Comprehension Questions

9. Where is the dining room? (7–8)
10. How close is the dining room to the sea? (8–10)
11. What is the view from each part of the dining room (the sides and front)? (11–12)
12. Standing in the dining room and looking back through the house, what is the order of rooms one would see? (12–13)

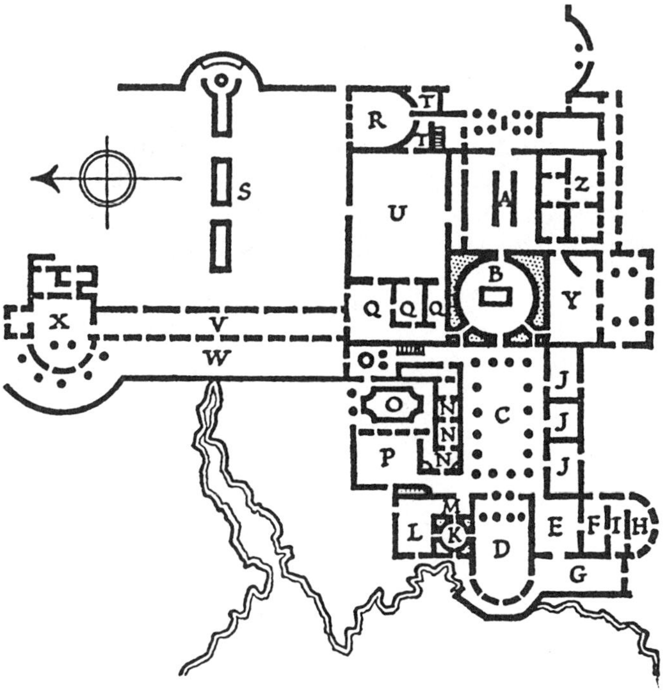

Ground plan of Pliny's Laurentine villa

THE PASSAGE AS A WHOLE FOR DISCUSSION

I.

Vīlla est ūsibus capāx, sed tūtēla nōn est sūmptuōsa. Est in prīmā parte vīllae ātrium frūgī nec tamen sordidum, deinde sunt porticūs in D litterae similitūdinem circumāctae, quae āream parvam sed fēstīvam inclūdunt. Hae porticūs sunt adversus tempestātēs receptāculum ēgregium; fenestrae et multō magis tēcta imminentia eās mūniunt.

II.

Est contrā mediās porticūs cavaedium hilare, mox est triclīnium satis pulchrum, quod in lītus excurrit; ac sī quandō Āfricus ventus mare impellit, triclīnium frāctī flūctūs leviter lavant. Undique triclīnium valvās aut fenestrās nōn minōrēs valvīs habet atque ita ab lateribus et ab fronte quasi tria maria prospectat; ab tergō respicit cavaedium, porticum, āream, porticum rūrsus, mox ātrium, silvās et longinquōs montēs.

Discussion Questions

1. Locate on the ground plan all of the rooms mentioned in the passage.
2. From Pliny's description of his **vīlla**, what is the impression one would get of the house itself and its surroundings?
3. Why was this **vīlla** especially pleasing to Pliny?
4. What words in Pliny's description of the **vīlla** emphasize its pleasantness and the pleasantness of its location?

Pliny continues describing the **vīlla** as follows. Locate each room on the plan, and follow the route that Pliny takes through the **vīlla**.

To the left of the dining room and a little farther back from the sea is a spacious bedroom [E], then another smaller one [F], which lets in the rising sun through one window and holds the setting sun through the other. From this window you can gaze out at the sea below, which is a safe distance away. The corner made by the wall of these bedrooms and the projecting wall of the dining room retains and intensifies the very clear sunlight. This area [G] is my favorite area in the winter and is the gymnasium for my household. Here the winds are all quiet, except those bringing rain clouds, and even these deprive the place of its serenity rather than its usefulness.

Around the corner there is a bedroom [H] curved in an apse, which follows the course of the sun through each of its windows. One of its walls has built-in shelves like a library, where I keep the books I like to read and reread. Next is a bedroom [I] with an intervening passage, which has a raised floor fitted with pipes to circulate hot steam at a healthy temperature. The rest of the rooms on this side of the house are occupied by my slaves and freedmen, and most of the rooms are neat enough to be shown to guests.

On the other side of the dining room is a very elegant bedroom [K]; then a room that can be either a large bedroom or a small dining room [L], which glows from the sun reflected from the sea. Behind this is a bedroom with an antechamber with height for coolness in summer and protection in winter, because it is protected from all the winds. A single wall separates this room from a similar bedroom and antechamber [M].

Next is the wide and spacious cold-room of the baths, which has two curved bathing basins on opposite walls [N]. These baths are spacious enough if you remember the sea is so close. Next are the oiling-room, furnace room, and hot-room for the bath, then two rooms, elegant but not expensive. Next is the wonderful swimming pool [O], from which the swimmers can see the sea. Not far is the ball-court [P], which receives the warmth of the setting sun. Here a tower rises, with two living rooms below and just as many above [Q], as well as a dining room that looks out upon the expanse of sea and shore and the charming villas.

There is another tower with a bedroom that lets in the rising and setting sun. Behind this are a wide storehouse and granary, with a dining room underneath [R], which receives only the sounds of the breaking waves of the sea—just a dying murmur. It looks out upon a garden [S] and a walkway enclosing the garden.

Discussion Questions

1. What are the advantages of the rooms to the left of the dining room?
2. Why has Pliny chosen this area of the house as his winter quarters? Be specific.
3. Describe the areas for bathing and swimming.
4. Identify the rooms contained in the two-story sections of the house.

Pliny is as pleased with the conveniences available at the location of his **vīlla** as he is with the house itself:

> Just one amenity and charm is missing from the house: running water. But it does have wells that are really springs since they are so near the surface of the ground. Certainly a surprising quality of this shore is that wherever you dig into the ground, ready and accessible water appears, which is clean and not spoiled by the nearby sea.
>
> The nearby woods supply enough firewood; the port of Ostia provides the other necessities. A village, which is just past the next house, can satisfy one's modest needs. In the village there are three baths for rent, a great convenience if perhaps a sudden arrival or a short stay makes you reluctant to heat the bath at home.
>
> The shore is adorned with a very pleasant variety of homes, some in groups and others spread far apart, which look like many cities from either the sea or shore. Sometimes the sand is too soft after a long period of good weather, but more often the repeated pounding of the waves hardens it. The sea does not provide fish of any value, but still it does contain the best sole and shrimp. Of course, our **vīlla** provides agricultural produce, especially milk, since the herds come here from the pastures whenever they need water and shade.

Discussion Questions

1. Where does Pliny get water for his house? Is that a problem?
2. Identify the various places Pliny would have to go to get provisions for his stay at the **vīlla**.
3. Describe the seashore as it would appear to someone in a boat off shore.

4
A PLEASANT RETREAT

Horace, *Letters* I.16

(with "The Roman Villa," Book 1, pages 35–38)

INTRODUCTION

For the life of Horace, see the introduction to Chapter 2, "Roman Roots in the Country." About six years after Horace had been introduced to Maecenas, Octavian's "minister of culture," Maecenas presented him with a country estate (**vīlla rūstica**), located thirty miles northeast of Rome in the ancestral territory of the Sabines. The Sabines were a people older than Rome itself, and from them, according to legend, Romulus, the founder of Rome, and his men carried off women to be their wives. The Romans also derived many religious practices from the Sabines.

The farm of a wealthy Roman citizen, or **vīlla rūstica,** as it was called in antiquity, typically provided its owner with a considerable income. Horace, however, regarded his Sabine farm rather differently. It was adequate for his support, but it was also a source of quiet pleasure and good health. For Horace this was "income" of another sort, but "income" nonetheless. The farm provided sufficient food for Horace, his slaves, and his animals. Situated in a shaded valley near the modern town of Licenza, it occupied fertile and secluded land with lush foliage and greenery. Horace, a city person and a sensitive poet, immediately appreciated the advantages afforded by his lovely Sabine farm, his retreat from the heat and noise of Rome.

In the following passage, taken from Horace's *Letters* I.16, the poet describes his Sabine farm. He highlights the natural aspects of the farm that appeal to him: the abundance of fruit and foliage; the mild climate; the cool, fresh water; and the quiet, safe solitude.

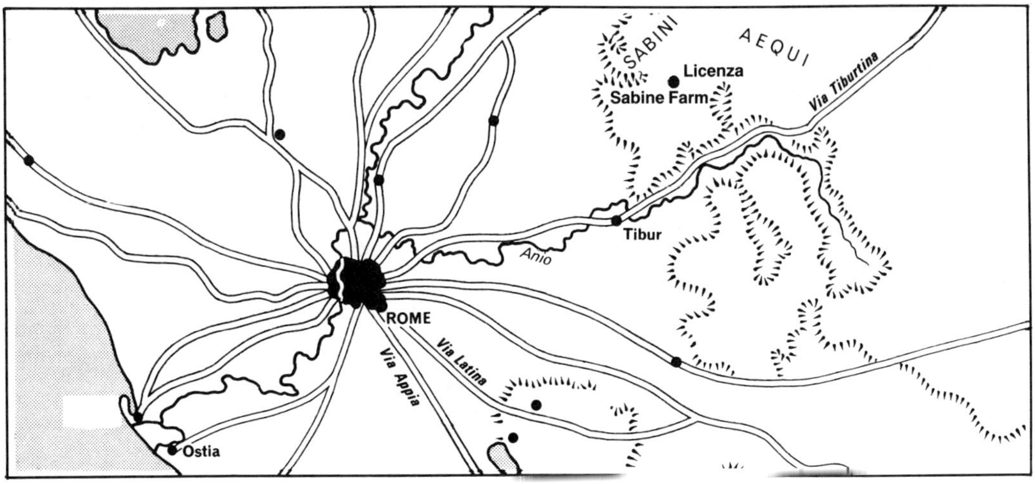

1 **fundus**, farm
optime Quīnctī, (my) best (dearest) Quinctius. We know only that he was a good friend of Horace.
arvō, with its plowland
dominus, master, head of a household, lord of an estate
pāscit, (it) feeds, supports
2 **opulentat**, (it) enriches
-que, and
olīvīs, with olives *or* with olive trees
pōmīs, with fruits *or* with fruit trees
prātīs, with meadows (for pasturing cattle)
ulmō (*fem.*), with an elm tree (used as a support for vines)
amictā, clothed, draped
vītibus, with grapevines
3 **scrībam**, I will write
tibi, to you
loquāciter, at length
dē fōrmā et sitū, about the appearance and location
agrī, of the land
montēs, the mountains
4 **continuus**, unbroken, continuous
opācus, shady
vallis, valley
dissociat, (it) separates
eōs, them (i.e., the mountains)
sōl, sun
veniēns, coming, rising
dextrum, right
5 **latus**, side
vallis, of the valley
aspicit, (it) looks at
discēdēns, departing, setting
laevum, left
currū fugiente, with its fleeing chariot (the sun is imagined as a golden chariot driven across the sky daily by Apollo)
6 **vapōrat**, (it) heats, warms
temperiem, mild climate
laudābis, you will praise

HORACE, *LETTERS* I.16

I.

Fundus meus, optime Quīnctī, arvō dominum pāscit opulentatque olīvīs, pōmīs, prātīs et ulmō amictā vītibus. Scrībam tibi loquāciter dē fōrmā et sitū agrī. Montēs nōn sunt continuī, sed opāca vallis dissociat eōs. Sōl veniēns dextrum latus vallis aspicit, discēdēns laevum latus currū fugiente vapōrat. Temperiem laudābis.

Comprehension Questions

1. In what two ways does Horace's farm benefit him? (1–2)
2. What does the farm produce? (2)
3. How will Horace write about his farm? (3)
4. What is the setting of the farm? (3–4)
5. On what does the sun shine when it is rising? (4–5)
6. On what does the sun shine when it is setting? (5–6)
7. What will Quinctius say about the climate? (6)

Ruins of the villa at Horace's Sabine farm

7 **benignus**, kind, beneficial, generous, abundant
veprēs, bramble bushes
rubicundus, red
corna, cornel berries, cornel cherries
prūna, plums
quercus, oak tree
8 **īlex**, holm oak
multā frūge, with much fruit, i.e., with many acorns
pecus, cattle, herd
multā umbrā, with much shade
dominus, master, head of a household, lord of an estate
iuvant, (they) help, benefit, please
fōns, spring
9 **etiam**, even
idōneus, suitable, large enough
dare, to give
rīvō, to the stream
Hebrus, the chief river of Thrace (**Thrācia**), north of Greece
nec . . . nec, neither . . . nor
frīgidior, colder
pūrior, purer
10 **ambit**, (it) goes around, winds through
aqua, water
īnfirmō capitī . . . ūtilis, useful (or beneficial) for a sick head
fluit, (it) flows
alvō, for the stomach
11 **hae latebrae**, these hiding places, this retreat (place "to get away from it all")
dulcēs, sweet, pleasant
crēdis mihi, you believe me
amoenus, delightful
12 **incolumem**, safe
tibi, for you
mē, me
praestant, (they) keep, preserve. The subject of the plural verb is **hae latebrae** in line 11.
Septembribus hōrīs, in the hours of September (i.e., in the heat at the end of the Italian summer)

II.

Benignī veprēs rubicunda corna et prūna ferunt. Quercus et īlex multā frūge pecus et multā umbrā dominum iuvant. Fōns est etiam idōneus dare nōmen rīvō; Hebrus nec frīgidior nec pūrior Thrāciam ambit. Aqua īnfirmō capitī fluit ūtilis et ūtilis alvō. Hae latebrae sunt dulcēs, etiam, si crēdis mihi, amoenae. Incolumem tibi mē praestant Septembribus hōrīs.

Comprehension Questions

8. How are the bramble bushes described? (7)
9. What do they produce? (7)
10. How do the oak trees benefit the cattle? (7–8) How do they benefit the master? (8)
11. How large is the spring? (8–9)
12. To what does Horace compare the stream coming from his spring? (9–10)
13. In what two ways is the stream coming from Horace's spring as good as or superior to the Hebrus River? (9–10)
14. For what does Horace especially value the water from the spring? (10)
15. In line 1 Horace refers to his farm with the word **fundus**. What different word does he use to refer to his farm at the beginning of line 11?
16. How does Horace describe his farm in line 11?
17. What benefit of the farm does Horace describe in line 12?

THE PASSAGE AS A WHOLE FOR DISCUSSION

I.

Fundus meus, optime Quīnctī, agrō dominum pāscit opulentatque olīvīs, pōmīs, prātīs et ulmō amictā vītibus. Scrībam tibi loquāciter dē fōrmā et sitū agrī. Montēs nōn sunt continuī, sed opāca vallis dissociat eōs. Sōl veniēns dextrum latus vallis aspicit, discēdēns laevum latus currū fugiente vapōrat. Temperiem laudābis.

II.

Benignī veprēs rubicunda corna et prūna ferunt. Quercus et īlex multā frūge pecus et multā umbrā dominum iuvant. Fōns est etiam idōneus dare nōmen rīvō; Hebrus nec frīgidior nec pūrior Thrāciam ambit. Aqua īnfirmō capitī fluit ūtilis et ūtilis alvō. Hae latebrae sunt dulcēs, etiam, si crēdis mihi, amoenae. Incolumem tibi mē praestant Septembribus hōrīs.

Discussion Questions

1. Judging from the two verbs (**pāscit** and **opulentat**) in the first sentence, what does Horace value about his farm? What different aspects or benefits of the farm does he mention in the last three sentences? (10–12)
2. Why is Horace so fond of the farm? List the specific things that make it attractive to him, citing the Latin nouns, adjectives, and verbs that give you this information.
3. Does Horace seem to be fond of his farm more for its practical, utilitarian benefits or for the personal pleasure that he takes in it? Justify your answer by referring to specific lines of the passage.
4. How does Horace's description of his farm differ from Pliny's description of his **vīlla** in the previous lesson? What different things does Pliny highlight in his letter?
5. How are the locations of the two country estates similar? How are they different?
6. How do the two writers feel about their country estates? For what different purposes do they use them?

5
SLAVES AND MASTERS IN ANCIENT ROME

Pliny, *Letters* III.14

(with "Treatment of Slaves," Book 1, pages 55–57)

INTRODUCTION

Pliny the Younger was born in A.D. 61 to a landowner in the municipality of Comum in northern Italy, but he was brought up by his uncle and adoptive father, whom we call Pliny the Elder. The uncle was a wealthy and politically active Roman with interests in biology, geology, medicine, and literature. Pliny the Younger became a successful lawyer and worked his way up the ladder of political offices (**cursus honōrum**). He served as the governor of the province of Bithynia in modern-day Turkey from A.D. 110 until his death in 112.

Pliny published nine books of letters and fully developed the letter as a distinct type of literature. These letters include news about social, domestic, judicial, and political events as well as advice, personal introductions, and commendations. Each of Pliny's letters is confined to a single subject. A letter may be written as a short essay, a character sketch, a miniature history, or a natural description. The letters document important facts of social history and reveal the life, tastes, and attitudes of upper-class Romans during the late first-century A.D.

The subject of our letter is the murder of Larcius Macedo by his slaves. Roman law regarded slaves as property (**rēs**), and as such they were subject to the unrestrained will of their masters, for they had no protection under the law. Although defined as property, slaves were intelligent beings with feelings. Their cooperation had to be obtained if they were to do their best work. Moreover, since Roman society was generally civilized and humane, public opinion did not sanction cruel treatment and abuse. Many slaves were treated kindly, and some even became friends of their masters.

Larcius Macedo is an example of the opposite extreme: his mistreatment of his slaves led to his being murdered. The punishment for crimes committed by slaves was severe. In the case of the murder of a master, it was Roman practice to put the entire household of slaves to death, even those innocent of taking part in the murder. Although the murder of a master by slaves was not frequent, the Roman aristocracy felt that a severe punishment was necessary, since some of their households included hundreds of slaves.

1 **praetōrius**, having the rank of **praetor**. A **praetor** was a Roman magistrate concerned chiefly with judicial functions.
erat, (he, she, it) was
superbus, haughty, proud
dominus, master
2 **saevus**, fierce, cruel
sē, himself
lavāre, to wash, bathe
Fōrmiānus, at Formiae, a city on the coast of Latium, a region of central Italy
repente, suddenly
3 **circumsistere**, to surround
alius . . . alius . . . alius, one . . . another . . . another
faucēs (*acc. pl.*), the throat
invādere, to assault, attack
ōs, face
verberāre, to beat, strike
4 **pectus**, chest
venter, belly, stomach
contundere, to pound to pieces
exanimis, lifeless, dead
putāre, to think
5 **abicere**, to throw aside
fervēns, hot, boiling
pavīmentum, tiled floor (of the baths). The floor would have been hot from the warmth of the furnaces below that were used to heat the water.
ille, he
sīve . . . sīve, either . . . or
quia, because
sentīre, to be conscious
6 **simulāre**, to pretend
immōbilis, motionless
extentus, stretched out
iacēre, to lie
7 **mortuus**, dead

PLINY, *LETTERS* III.14

I.

Larcius Macedō, vir praetōrius, erat superbus dominus et saevus. Sē lavat in vīllā Fōrmiānā et repente eum servī circumsistunt. Alius faucēs invādit, alius ōs verberat, alius pectus et ventrem contundit. Ubi servī eum exanimem putant, abiciunt in fervēns pavīmentum. Ille, sīve quia nōn sentit, sīve quia sē nōn sentīre simulat, immōbilis et extentus iacet, sed nōn est mortuus.

Comprehension Questions

1. What rank was Larcius Macedo? (1)
2. What kind of master was he? (1–2)
3. Where is he bathing? (2)
4. What do his slaves suddenly do? (2–3)
5. How is he assaulted? (3–4)
6. Where do the slaves throw him when they think he is lifeless? (4–5)
7. What two possible explanations are given for why Larcius Macedo continues to appear lifeless? (5–6)
8. What would make the slaves think that he might be dead? (6)
9. Was he indeed dead? (6–7)

8 **dēmum**, finally
quasi exanimātus, as if (merely) out of breath, as if (he had merely) fainted
efferunt, (they) carry out
excipere, to receive
9 **fīdēliōrēs**, more faithful, more loyal
concubīna, concubine, a slave woman who sometimes shares her master's bed
cum (+ *abl.*), with
ululātus, yelling, wailing
concurrere, to run or rush up
10 **dominus**, master
oculus, eye
tollere, to raise
corpus, body
-que, and
agitāre, to move, stir
incipere, to begin
tūtus, safe
11 **diffugere**, to run away, scatter

12 **quot**, how many
perīcula, dangers
contumēlia, outrage, affront, insult
lūdibria, insults
patimur, we endure, suffer
nec, and not, nor
13 **possumus**, we can, are able
sēcūrus, free from care, safe
etiam sī, even if
remissus, relaxed, easy-going
mītis, kind, mild, gentle
quia, because
14 **iūstus**, just, fair
necāre, to kill

II.

Tum dēmum eum quasi exanimātum efferunt; excipiunt eum servī fidēliōrēs, concubīnae cum ululātū et clāmōre concurrunt. Dominus oculōs tollere corpusque agitāre incipit (iam tūtum est). Diffugiunt servī.

The master dies a few days later, but he dies avenged because most of the slaves are captured and put to death before he dies. Pliny laments the precarious position of masters:

Quot perīcula, quot contumēliās, quot lūdibria patimur! Nec possumus esse sēcūrī, etiam sī remissī et mītēs sumus, quia servī nōn iūstī sed scelestī sunt et igitur dominōs necant.

Comprehension Questions

10. What do the slaves who beat Larcius Macedo finally do with him? (8)
11. Who receive him? (8–9)
12. What is the reaction of his concubines? (9)
13. What does the master begin to do? (10)
14. Why is he now able to show signs of life? (10)
15. What do the slaves do now? (11)
16. What does Pliny complain that masters must endure? (12)
17. What is it not possible for masters to be? (12–13)
18. What explanation does Pliny give for why slaves kill their masters? (14)

THE PASSAGE AS A WHOLE FOR DISCUSSION

I.

Larcius Macedō, vir praetōrius, erat superbus dominus et saevus. Sē lavat in vīllā Fōrmiānā et repente eum servī circumsistunt. Alius faucēs invādit, alius ōs verberat, alius pectus et ventrem contundit. Ubi servī eum exanimem putant, abiciunt in fervēns pavīmentum. Ille, sīve quia nōn sentit, sīve quia sē nōn sentīre simulat, immōbilis et extentus iacet, sed nōn est mortuus.

II.

Tum dēmum eum quasi exanimātum efferunt; excipiunt eum servī fidēliōrēs, concubīnae cum ululātū et clāmōre concurrunt. Dominus oculōs tollere corpusque agitāre incipit (iam tūtum est). Diffugiunt servī.

The master dies a few days later, but he dies avenged because most of the slaves are captured and put to death before he dies. Pliny laments the precarious position of masters:

Quot perīcula, quot contumēliās, quot lūdibria patimur! Nec possumus esse sēcūrī, etiam sī remissī et mītēs sumus, quia servī nōn iūstī sed scelestī sunt et igitur dominōs necant.

Discussion Questions

A. Pliny's attitude toward slavery:

1. Does Pliny approve of Larcius Macedo's treatment of his slaves? What words tell you whether he does or does not?
2. Does he approve of the slaves murdering their master? What words tell you?
3. How do lines 12–14 reflect Pliny's upper-class values? What stereotypes or prejudices do they reveal?
4. To what extent does it appear that Pliny's indignation, outrage, and concern are justified?
5. Do you think Pliny is a humane person?

B. Pliny's abilities as a storyteller:

1. In lines 2 and following, Pliny suddenly shifts from a narrative past tense (**erat**, "he was," line 1) to the present tense. How

does this make the actions that are being described seem more vivid?

2. How is this shift appropriate to the sense of the narrative?
3. What interesting details does Pliny include to make the story dramatic?
4. Find two places where Pliny includes three parallel clauses or phrases in the same sentence. Can you think of any reasons why such grouping of items by threes is especially effective?
5. Why do you think Pliny's subject matter was newsworthy to his friends?
6. How is our interest in the story different from the interest Pliny's friends would have taken in it?

A slave sharpening a knife

6
SENECA
ON SLAVERY AND FREEDOM

Seneca, *Moral Letters* XLVII

(with "Treatment of Slaves," Book 1, pages 55–57)

INTRODUCTION

Seneca was born in about 4 B.C. at Corduba in southern Spain. He was born into a middle-class family that had come from Italy as administrators and soldiers. Seneca became interested in philosophy at an early age; he was eventually attracted to Stoicism, and he became one of its leading exponents during the early Empire.

When Seneca went to Rome is not known, but once he was there he wrote many treatises, which won him not only renown but also the enmity of the emperor Gaius Caligula, who banished Seneca in A.D. 41 because of jealousy. In A.D. 49 Seneca was recalled to Rome at the request of Agrippina (mother of Nero, the emperor-to-be). In A.D. 51 he was appointed tutor to the young Nero, and in A.D. 54 he became the political advisor of Nero (now emperor).

Seneca acted as advisor to the young emperor for a number of years; he retired from this position in A.D. 62, after the death of his long-time co-advisor, Burrus, who was prefect of the palace guard. Seneca devoted the few remaining years of his life to the pursuit of philosophy. In A.D. 65 he was ordered by the emperor Nero to commit suicide for his alleged participation in a conspiracy to assassinate Nero and make Piso emperor. Throughout his adult life, Seneca had followed and expounded the Stoic philosophy, and he died with calm, philosophic resolve.

The word *stoic* is derived from the name of a public hall or portico in Athens, the *Stoa Poikile* ("Painted Portico"), in which Zeno, the founder of a philosophical sect, and his successors taught in the late fourth and early third centuries B.C. Early Stoic doctrine was divided into three parts:

1. Physics, the study of natural science
2. Logic, the theory of knowledge, thought, and rhetoric
3. Ethics, the study of human behavior

The basic premises of Stoicism were the following:

1. Since virtue is based on knowledge, one should pursue knowledge with the goal of increasing virtue.
2. It is the aim of the philosopher to live in harmony with nature. Reason was identified with God and thought of as a guiding principle that directs human beings to live according to nature.
3. To be virtuous, that is, to live in harmony with nature, as revealed by reason, is the only good; not to be virtuous is the only evil.
4. There is an underlying unity in humankind. All humans are born in the same way; all are born with the same faculties and senses. The Stoics, therefore, expounded the idea of a human community based on what was termed the "seed of reason" that was believed to have been sown in each and every human being.

During Seneca's lifetime, the Stoic thinkers were most interested in ethical topics, particularly the humanity shared by all peoples—slaves and masters, men and women.

Seneca enlarged on this theme of unity. He felt that regardless of what position in society Fate assigned to individuals, all people were human beings and should be treated accordingly.

All of Seneca's letters are addressed to a young man named Lucilius, whom he was helping to train in Stoic philosophy. The following extracts from letter XLVII begin with the topic of how slaves should be treated and then raise larger issues of freedom and slavery. You are in for some surprises, for Seneca will show that slaves may be free and that all humans are slaves.

Bust, perhaps of Seneca the philosopher

1 **libenter**, gladly, with pleasure
eīs, those (people)
ab tē, from your house
cognōscere, to learn
familiāriter, on friendly terms
cum (+ *abl.*), with
2 **vīvere**, to live
hoc, this fact
prūdentia, good sense, prudence
ērudītiō, instruction, cultivation, education
decet, (it) befits, is in keeping with

3 **immō**, on the contrary, no indeed, rather
hominēs, men
4 **contubernālēs**, comrades, buddies
humilis, humble

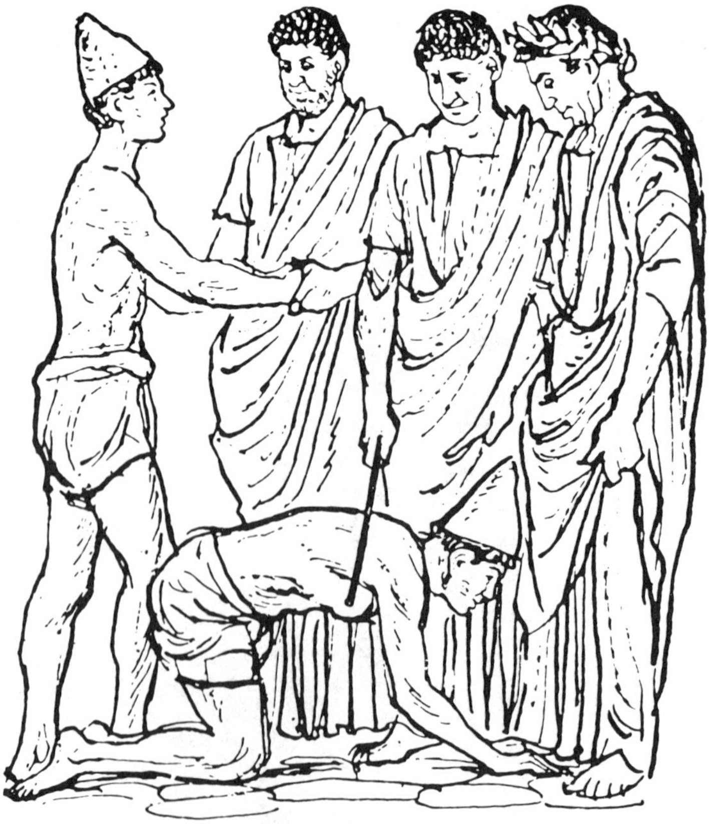

Slave being given the cap of freedom

SENECA, *MORAL LETTERS* XLVII

I.

Libenter ex eīs, quī ab tē veniunt, cognōscō tē familiāriter cum servīs tuīs vīvere. Hoc prūdentiam tuam, hoc ērudītiōnem decet.

Comprehension Questions

1. For what is Seneca praising Lucilius? (1–2)
2. What kind of a man is Lucilius? (2)

II.

"Servī sunt!" Immō hominēs! "Servī sunt!" Immō contubernālēs! "Servī sunt!" Immō humilēs amīcī!

In the above passage Seneca is using a literary device known as the imaginary interlocutor. By having this interlocutor play the role of devil's advocate, Seneca turns the letter into a dramatic dialogue or debate. Seneca defends an enlightened position against the voice of common opinion (that of the imaginary interlocutor).

Comprehension Question

3. In reply to the imaginary interlocutor, what three things does Seneca say that slaves are?

5 **cōgitāre**, to think about, ponder
iste, that one, he
vocāre, to call
ex eīsdem sēminibus, from the same seed
6 **nātus est**, (he) has been born
eōdem caelō (*abl.*), the same sky
fruitur (+ *abl.*), (he) enjoys
aequē, equally, just as you do
spīrāre, to breathe
vīvere, to live
7 **moritur**, (he) dies
fortasse, perhaps
līber, free
animō, in (his) heart, mind
8 **hoc**, this
illī, to him
nocet, (it) does harm to . . .
ostendere, to show
alius . . . alius (9) . . . **alius**, one . . . another . . . another
libīdinī, to (his) desire, longing, lust
9 **servīre**, to be a slave (to)
avāritiae, to (his) greed, avarice
ambitiōnī, to (his) ambition, striving for popularity
timōrī, to fear

10 **clēmenter**, gently, mercifully, compassionately
cōmiter, politely, courteously, kindly
quoque, also
sermō, conversation, talk
11 **illum**, him
admittere, to admit
cōnsilium, deliberation, planning
convīctus, association, socializing, banquet
haec, these things
agere, to do
12 **colitur**, (he) is cultivated, honored
amātur, (he) is loved
amor, love
cum (+ *abl.*), with
timor, fear
miscērī, to be mixed

III.

Cōgitā! Iste, quem servum tuum vocās, ex eīsdem sēminibus nātus est, eōdem caelō fruitur, aequē spīrat, aequē vīvit, aequē moritur! "Servus est!" Sed fortasse est līber animō. "Servus est!" Hoc illī nocet? Ostende! Quis nōn est servus? Alius libīdinī servit, alius avāritiae, alius ambitiōnī, omnēs timōrī.

Comprehension Questions

4. In what five ways are slaves said to be equal to free men? (5–7)
5. In what way may a slave perhaps be, in fact, free? (7)
6. Does Seneca believe that the status of servitude is in itself necessarily harmful to the slave? (8)
7. In what four ways are slaves and free men in fact alike? (8–9)

IV.

Vīve cum servō clēmenter, cōmiter quoque, et in sermōnem illum admitte et in cōnsilium et in convīctum. Quī haec agit, colitur et amātur; nōn potest amor cum timōre miscērī.

Comprehension Questions

8. In what two ways does Seneca advise Lucilius to live with his slave? (10)
9. Into what three things should Lucilius admit his slave? (10–11)
10. What will be the result if Lucilius follows Seneca's advice? (11–12)
11. What will be lost if the relationship between slave and master is based on fear? (12)
12. How do you think the Romans, in general, would have viewed the opinions proposed in this letter?

THE PASSAGE AS A WHOLE FOR INTERPRETIVE READING

Since this passage is a kind of dramatic dialogue, it provides an ideal opportunity for oral reading and interpretation. Practice reading the passage aloud. Put yourself into the character of Seneca (the main voice) and into the very different character of the imaginary interlocutor. Decide what tone of voice to use for each role. Vary your tone for each of the roles as the dialogue moves along. Which sentences should be read with a tone of indignation and outrage? Which with a tone of calm reason? Be ready to "perform" the passage in front of your class.

I.

Libenter ex eīs, quī ab tē veniunt, cognōscō tē familiāriter cum servīs tuīs vīvere. Hoc prūdentiam tuam, hoc ērudītiōnem decet.

II.

"Servī sunt!" Immō hominēs! "Servī sunt!" Immō contubernālēs! "Servī sunt!" Immō humilēs amīcī!

III.

Cogitā! Iste, quem servum tuum vocās, ex eīsdem sēminibus nātus est, eōdem caelō fruitur, aequē spīrat, aequē vīvit, aequē moritur! "Servus est!" Sed fortasse est līber animō. "Servus est!" Hoc illī nocet? Ostende! Quis nōn est servus? Alius libīdinī servit, alius avāritiae, alius ambitiōnī, omnēs timōrī.

IV.

Vīve cum servō clēmenter, cōmiter quoque, et in sermōnem illum admitte et in cōnsilium et in convīctum. Quī haec agit, colitur et amātur; nōn potest amor cum timōre miscērī.

7
THE RESPONSIBILITIES OF A FARM MANAGER

Cato, *On Agriculture* V.1–5

(after Chapter 12)

INTRODUCTION

Marcus Porcius Cato the Elder, who lived from 234 to 149 B.C., was called the father of Latin prose. He had an extensive political career, serving as consul in 195 and as censor in 184. He was elected to the censorship at a time when the public had lost confidence in the character of their political leaders and when the influence of the Greeks and of Eastern religions was growing. Cato symbolized the customs of the ancestors (**mōrēs maiōrum**) of the Romans. He was conservative and severe in administering the censorship.

Cato wrote speeches, treatises, and a history of Rome. In the *De agri cultura* (*On Agriculture*), written in 160 B.C., Cato gives shrewd advice for Romans who want to make farming their business. He describes how one should shop for a farm and how to administer it. Consistent with his promotion of the simple life, he reminds his readers that their ancestors praised farmers because they were the bravest and heartiest of men.

The following passage lists the responsibilities of the farm manager (**vīlicus**). The **vīlicus** was a slave or freedman appointed by the owner to manage his estate. Most likely, he would have grown up on a farm and would be of healthy physique and cooperative disposition.

Mosaic showing a Roman farm with pheasants, geese, and ducks

1 **haec**, these things
officia, duties
disciplīna, -ae (*f*), discipline
ūtitur (+ *abl.*), (he) uses, employs
fēriae, -ārum (*f pl*), holy days, religious festivals
servō, servāre (1), to keep, observe
2 **aliēnō** (*abl.*), that which belongs to another
manum, hand
abstineō, abstinēre (2) (+ *acc.* and *abl.*), to keep . . . away from . . .
sua, his own things
dīligenter, carefully
quis, anyone
quid, anything
3 **dēlinquō, dēlinquere** (3), to do . . . wrong
prō (+ *abl.*), in proportion, according to
noxa, -ae (*f*), injurious act, fault, crime
modus, -ī (*m*), way, manner, measure
vindicō, vindicāre (1), to punish
videt nē . . . male sit, he sees to it that there is no harm to. . . .
familiae, to the family (of slaves in the household). Note that the word **familia** is used in this passage to refer to the household slaves as a group and not to the master's immediate family.
4 **nē algeat**, that (it) is not cold
nē ēsuriat, that (it) is not hungry
opere . . . exercet, (he) keeps (them) busy with work
bene, well, very
facilius, more easily
5 **malō** (*abl.*), wrongdoing
prohibeō, prohibēre (2) (+ *abl.*), to hold . . . back from . . .
male facere, to act wickedly, do wrong. I.e., "for the **familia** to. . . . "
6 **patitur**, (he) allows
7 **illum**, him
pūniō, punīre (4), to punish
beneficiō (*abl.*), good deed, kindness
grātiam rēfert, (he) returns thanks, shows gratitude
aliīs, to others
rēctē, rightly, properly. Note that **rēctē facere** is the opposite of **male facere** (see lines 5 and 6).
8 **libet** (+ *dat.*), it is pleasing (to) . . . , they want

CATO, *ON AGRICULTURE* V.1–5

I.

Haec sunt vīlicī officia. Disciplīnā bonā ūtitur. Fēriās servat. Aliēnō manum abstinet, sua servat dīligenter. Sī quis quid dēlinquit, prō noxā bonō modō vindicat. Videt nē familiae male sit, nē algeat, nē ēsuriat. Familiam opere bene exercet; facilius malō et aliēnō prohibet. Vīlicus sī nōn vult male facere, familia nōn male facit. Sī vīlicus familiam male facere patitur, dominus illum pūnit. Sī prō beneficiō grātiam rēfert, aliīs rēctē facere libet.

Comprehension Questions

1. What must a **vīlicus** use in administering his position? (1)
2. What does he observe? (1)
3. How does he regard the property of others? (2) How does he regard his own property? (2)
4. How does he punish wrongdoers? (3)
5. What responsibilities does he shoulder for the household slaves? (3–4)
6. How does he keep them from wrongdoing and theft? (4–5)
7. What happens if the **vīlicus** does not do wrong? (5–6)
8. Who is punished if the household slaves do wrong? (6–7)
9. What happens if the **vīlicus** shows gratitude for a deed well done? (7–8)

9 **nōn dēbet esse**, (he) must not be
ambulātor, ambulātōris (*m*), one who walks about doing nothing, a loafer
sobrius, sober
10 **cēna, -ae** (*f*), dinner
nēquō, not to any place, nowhere
it, he goes
familia, -ae (*f*), household slaves
exerceō, exercēre (2), to keep busy
11 **imperō, imperāre** (1), to command, order
12 **opus rūsticum omne**, all the farm work (i.e., all of the different kinds of work on the farm)
sciō, scīre (4), to know how
id, it
13 **lassus**, weary, tired, exhausted
fierī, to become
intellegō, intellegere (3), to understand
mēns, mentis (*f*), mind, reason, feeling
14 **illī**, they
animus, -ī (*m*), mind, spirit
  animō aequiōre, with a calmer, more patient, more contented spirit
15 **prīmus**, first
cubitū (*abl.*), lying down, bed
surgō, surgere (3) (+ *abl.*), to rise, get up (from)
postrēmus, last
cubitum, to bed, to sleep
prius, first
ut, that
16 **clausa sit**, be closed, shut
suō . . . locō, in his or her own place
quisque, each one, everyone
cubō, cubāre (1), to lie down, sleep
iūmenta, beasts of burden, cattle
17 **pābulum**, food, fodder

II.

Vīlicus nōn dēbet esse ambulātor. Sobrius esse semper dēbet. Ad cēnam nēquō it. Familiam exercet, et familia igitur omnia, quae dominus imperat, facit.

Vīlicus opus rūsticum omne facere scit et id facit saepe sed nōn lassus fierī dēbet. Sī opus omne facit, intellegit mentem familiae, et illī animō aequiōre faciunt.

Prīmus cubitū surgit, postrēmus cubitum it. Prius videt ut vīlla clausa sit et ut suō quisque locō cubet et ut iūmenta pābulum habeant.

Comprehension Questions

10. What is a **vīlicus** not allowed to be? (9)
11. What must the **vīlicus** always be? (9)
12. Where must he never go? (10)
13. What results from his keeping the household slaves busy? (10–11)
14. What must the **vīlicus** know how to do? (12)
15. To what extent should he himself actually do farm work? (12–13)
16. For what two reasons should he do farm work himself? (13–14)
17. When does the **vīlicus** arise? (15) When does he go to bed? (15)
18. What three things must he see to before he goes to bed? (15–17)

A peasant going to market with a cow, a pig, two lambs, and a basket of fruit

THE PASSAGE AS A WHOLE FOR DISCUSSION

I.

Haec sunt vīlicī officia. Disciplīnā bonā ūtitur. Fēriās servat. Aliēnō manum abstinet, sua servat dīligenter. Sī quis quid dēlinquit, prō noxā bonō modō vindicat. Videt nē familiae male sit, nē algeat, nē ēsuriat. Familiam opere bene exercet; facilius malō et aliēnō prohibet. Vīlicus sī nōn vult male facere, familia nōn male facit. Sī vīlicus familiam male facere patitur, dominus illum pūnit. Sī prō beneficiō grātiam rēfert, aliīs rēctē facere libet.

II.

Vīlicus nōn dēbet esse ambulātor. Sobrius esse semper dēbet. Ad cēnam nēquō it. Familiam exercet, et familia igitur omnia, quae dominus imperat, facit.

Vīlicus opus rūsticum omne facere scit et id facit saepe sed nōn lassus fierī dēbet. Sī opus omne facit, intellegit mentem familiae, et illī animō aequiōre faciunt.

Prīmus cubitū surgit, postrēmus cubitum it. Prius videt ut vīlla clausa sit et ut suō quisque locō cubet et ut iūmenta pābulum habeant.

Discussion Questions

1. What two key words in the first line set the tone of the passage as a whole?
2. What are the farm manager's responsibilities? Make a list of them.
3. What special privilege might one expect him to get that he is specifically denied?
4. How is he to exercise control over the household slaves? How does he keep them in line? How does he keep them contented ?
5. What is the relationship between the farm manager and the master?
6. What can you conclude from this passage about the treatment of farm slaves?
7. What can you conclude from this passage about the overall organization of labor on Roman farms? Does the hierarchy of authority seem to have been stable? Do those at the various levels seem to have been content with their lot?

8
STOPPING AT AN INN

Erasmus, *Colloquies*, "Inns"

(after Chapter 18)

INTRODUCTION

Erasmus of Rotterdam was one of the great scholars and churchmen of Northern Europe during the period of the revival of classical learning known as the Renaissance. He lived from 1466 to 1536 and was thus a younger contemporary of Christopher Columbus (1451–1506). Erasmus edited many works of Greek and Latin authors and of the early Church fathers, and he translated the Greek New Testament into Latin, which was the language of learning and scholarship throughout Europe at this time.

Erasmus was known for his wit and humor in addition to his learning. He was a teacher as well as a scholar, and he wrote a series of Latin dialogues titled *Colloquia familiaria*, known in English as the *Colloquies* (or one might call them *Everyday Conversations*). These were intended to instruct the young in the niceties of the Latin language, but at the same time they contain entertaining, humorous, and often satirical observations on a wide variety of types of people and styles of life.

The *Colloquy* from which the following passage is taken is titled *Diversoria* (*Inns*), and the conversation turns on a contrast between French and German inns. French inns are pleasant and full of good cheer, superb food, witty conversation, and women who offer irresistible hospitality; German inns are the opposite in every way.

We can only imagine what ancient Roman wayside inns were like, but they do not appear to have had a good reputation. Ancient writers speak of people "lurking around" in inns and of inns as unsavory places; innkeepers are described as "stingy," and the naturalist Pliny refers to vermin found in inns in the summer that bother you with their sudden jumping and to others that get into your hair. Cicero tells the story of the Greek innkeeper who murdered one of his guests (see ECCE ROMANI, Chapter 20), and Horace's description of his journey from Rome to Brundisium (see ECCE ROMANI, Book 2, pages 22–24) contains several unflattering references to innkeepers and wayside inns.

The following passage from Erasmus gives his unflattering description of an inn in Germany.

1 **advenientem**, a person arriving
aliquis, someone
2 **fenestra, -ae** (*f*), window
dīcō, dīcere (3), to say
licet, it is allowed, you are permitted
3 **sit**, (it) is
stabulum, -ī (*n*), stable
mōnstrō, mōnstrāre, to show
intrāns, entering
4 **hypocaustum, -ī** (*n*), stove room
ocrea, -ae (*f*), leggings (cloth or leather coverings to protect the lower legs)
sarcina, -ae (*f*), baggage
lutum, -ī (*n*), mud
aqua, -ae (*f*), water
5 **lavō, lavāre**, to wash
sordidior, dirtier (than + *abl.*)
parvus, -a, -um, small
6 **conveniō, convenīre** (3), to come together, gather
octōgintā, eighty
aut, or
nōnāgintā, ninety
pedes, peditis (*m*), foot soldier
7 **eques, equitis** (*m*), soldier who fights from horseback
mercātor, mercātōris (*m*), merchant
nauta, -ae (*m*), sailor
aurīga, -ae (*m*), charioteer
agricola, -ae (*m*), farmer
fēmina, -ae (*f*), woman
8 **sānus, -a, -um**, healthy
aegrōtus, -a, -um, sick
  sānī, aegrōtī: adjectives used as nouns

ERASMUS, *COLLOQUIES*, "INNS"

I.

Advenientem nēmō salūtat. Sī diū clāmās, aliquis per fenestram spectat. Sī nōn "Abī" dīcit, licet intrāre. Sī rogās ubi sit stabulum, manū mōnstrat. In caupōnam intrāns, venīs in hypocaustum cum ocreīs, sarcinīs, lutō. Aqua est, sī vīs manūs lavāre, sed est sordidior lutō. Saepe in ūnum parvum hypocaustum conveniunt octōgintā aut nōnāgintā, peditēs, equitēs, mercātōrēs, nautae, aurīgae, agricolae, puerī, fēminae, sānī, aegrōtī.

Comprehension Questions

1. How are guests greeted upon their arrival at the inn? (1)
2. What does a guest have to do to get any attention at all? (1–2)
3. How does a guest learn whether he or she may enter or not? (2)
4. What is inhospitable about the way the innkeeper shows where the stable is? (2–3)
5. What do the guests bring into the stove room with them? (4)
6. Are the guests able to wash up satisfactorily? If so, why? If not, why not? (4–5)
7. How many different kinds of people gather in the stove room of the inn? (6–8)

9 **barbātus, -a, -um,** bearded
mēnsa, -ae (*f*), table
10 **appōnō, appōnere** (3), to set down
pinācium, -ī (*n*), plate
cochleāre, cochleāris (*n*), spoon
ligneus, -a, -um, wooden
cyathus -ī (*m*), pitcher
vitreus, -a, -um, made of glass
11 **vīnum, -ī** (*n*), wine
ācer, ācris, ācre, sharp, bitter
pānis, pānis (*m*), bread
puls, pultis (*f*), porridge
fictus, -a, -um, fake, amateur
mōriō, mōriōnis (*m*), jester, clown
12 **saltō** (1), to jump, dance
13 **loquentem,** speaking, talking
dōnec, until
14 **quam,** than
15 **linteum, -ī** (*n*), bed sheet
forte, perhaps
lōtus, -a, -um, washed
ante sex mēnsēs, six months ago
16 **placent,** they are pleasing

II.

Ubi tempus est cēnāre, homō barbātus mēnsās parat et appōnit pinācium et cochleāre ligneum, cyathum vitreum cum vīnō ācrī, pānem et pultēs. Adveniunt fictī mōriōnēs, quī cantant, clāmant, saltant. Magnī sunt clāmor et fragor. Nēmō alterum loquentem audīre potest. Cubitum īre nōn potes dōnec omnēs volunt. Ubi intrās cubiculum, nihil aliud invenīs quam lectum cum linteīs forte lōtīs ante sex mēnsēs. Sī lintea sordida reprehendis, caupō, "Sī nōn placent," inquit, "pete aliam caupōnam."

Comprehension Questions

8. What feature of the man who sets the table might be considered unpleasant? (9)
9. What is "cheap" about the place settings? (10)
10. How pleasing is the food and drink that is offered? (11)
11. What would some guests find objectionable about the entertainment? (11–13)
12. What is the rule about the time when you can go to bed? (13–14)
13. What are the only things you find in your bedroom? (14–15)
14. What might you find objectionable about the bed sheets? (15)
15. What is the answer if you complain? (16–17)

DISCUSSION

On the next page is a picture of a Roman inn beside a country road. Some guests have just arrived in a two-wheeled cart. The innkeeper is welcoming them with a glass of wine. Guests need a bath after a long day's traveling, and a slave can be seen to the right of the picture, stoking the boiler that heats water for the bathhouse.

Discussion Questions

1. In what ways does the inn shown on the next page seem to be a more pleasant place to stay than the inn described by Erasmus?
2. In what ways would a night's stay at Erasmus' inn be different from a night's stay at a modern motel?

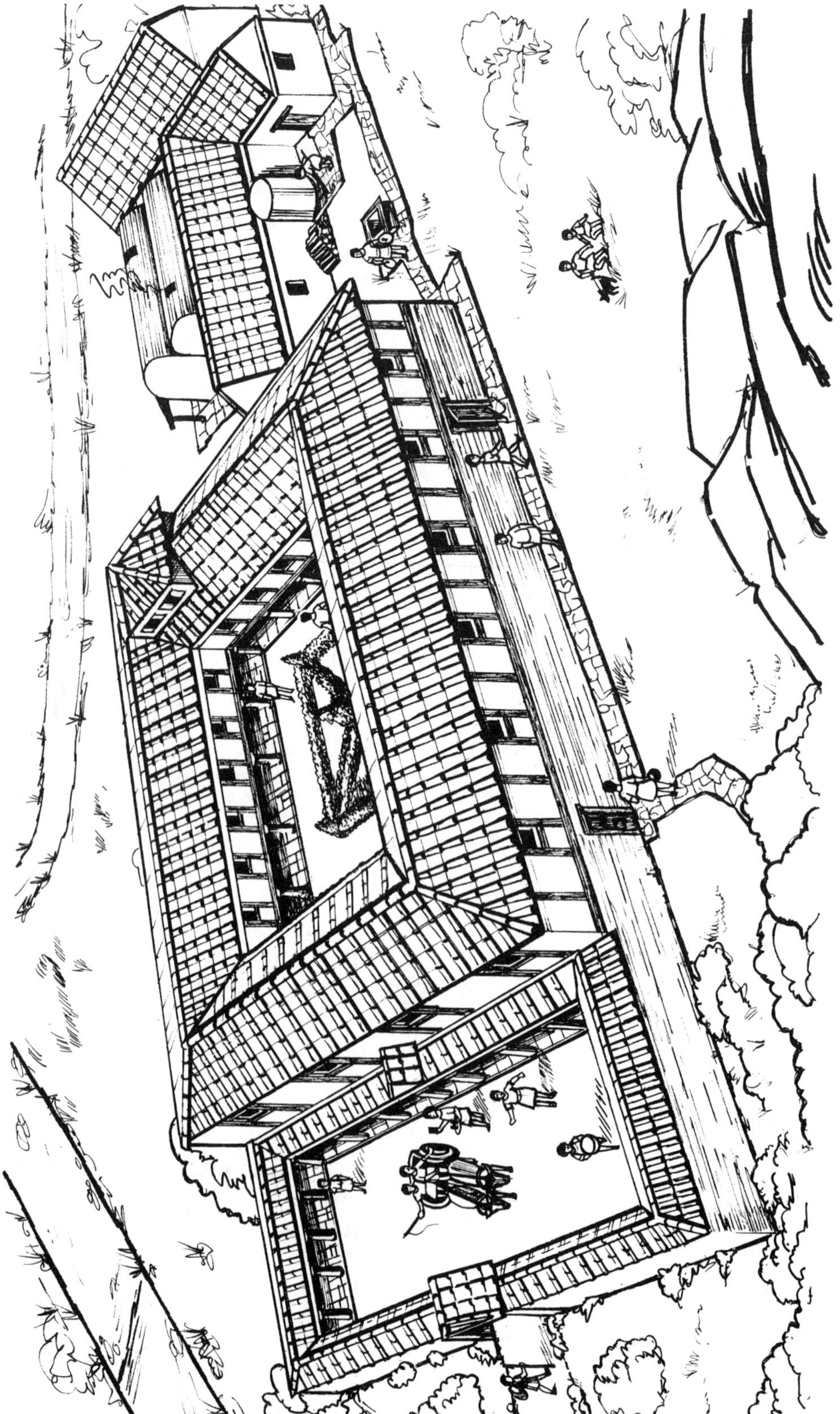

A Roman country inn

9
GHOSTS

Pliny, *Letters* VII.27

(after Chapter 20)

INTRODUCTION

For Pliny and his *Letters*, see Chapter 3, "Pliny's Laurentine Villa," and Chapter 5, "Slaves and Masters in Ancient Rome." In the present letter, Pliny is asking his friend Licinius Sura whether he thinks ghosts really exist or are merely figments of our imagination. Pliny says that stories he has heard make him lean toward believing that ghosts do exist. One story concerned a certain Curtius Rufus, who when he was serving on the governor's staff in Africa saw a ghost in the form of a woman who foretold his future—that he would return to Rome, hold a public office there, and then return to Africa where he would die; all of these things came true. Pliny also tells about two of his slaves who dreamed that patches of their hair were cut off by mysterious figures dressed in white and in the morning found that their hair had actually been shorn.

Pliny asks his friend to consider in particular a story that he has heard about a haunted house in Athens. In the middle of the night metalic sounds and the rattling of chains would be heard and a ghost would appear, with chains bound around his wrists and legs. The occupants of the house were so terrified by the repeated appearances of the ghost that they deserted the house and put it up for sale. A philosopher from abroad, named Athenodorus, came to Athens and, knowing nothing about the ghost, sought to rent the house. He became suspicious because of the low price that was being asked, and he found out that the house was haunted. This did not deter him but actually made him all the more eager to rent the house, because as a philosopher or "lover of wisdom" he wanted to find out the truth of the matter. The Latin passage in this lesson tells what happened the first night he spent in the house.

1 **coepit**, it began
2 **domūs**, of the house
dīmittō, dīmittere (3), **dīmīsī, dīmissum**, to send away
3 **simulācrum, -ī** (*n*), ghost
4 **prīmum**, at first
ferrum, -ī (*n*), iron
vincula, -ōrum (*n pl*), chains
5 **sonantia**, making a noise, rattling
oculus, -ī (*m*), eye
tollō, tollere (3), **sustulī, sublātum**, to lift, raise, pick up
offirmō (1), to make firm, steel (one's mind)
6 **pergō, pergere** (3), **perrēxī, perrēctum**, to continue
crēbrēscō, crēbrēscere (3), **crēbuī**, to increase
7 **respiciō, respicere** (3), **respexī, respectum**, to look back, look back at
quiētē, quietly, calmly
8 **invītō** (1), to invite, beckon
9 **reveniō, revenīre** (4), **revēnī, reventum**, to return
timēns, fearing

PLINY, *LETTERS* VII.27

I.

Ubi coepit advesperāscere, Athēnodōrus iussit servōs lectum movēre in prīmam domūs partem. Tum servōs dīmīsit. Ipse epistulam scrībere coepit, quod dē simulācrīs cōgitāre nōlēbat. Prīmum erat silentium noctis. Deinde audīvit ferrum et vincula sonantia. Ille oculōs nōn sustulit sed animum offirmāvit et scrībere perrēxit. Tum fragor crēbuit et appropinquāvit. Athēnodōrus respexit, vīdit et agnōvit simulācrum, quod quiētē stābat et manū invītābat Athēnodōrum. Ille tamen nōn īvit sed revēnit ad epistulam, nōn timēns simulācrum.

Comprehension Questions

1. What two things did Athenodorus do at nightfall? (1–2)
2. Why did he begin to write a letter? (2–3)
3. What did he hear in the dead of night? (4–5)
4. What was his reaction? (5–6)
5. What finally made him turn and look? (6–7)
6. What was the ghost doing? (7–8)
7. What was Athenodorus' reaction? (8–9)

10 **simulācrum, -ī** (*n*), ghost
caput, capitis (*n*), head
sonō (1), to make a noise
11 **respiciō, respicere** (3), **respexī, respectum**, to look back, look back at
rūrsus, again
12 **invītō** (1), to invite, beckon
lūmen, lūminis (*n*), lamp
tollō, tollere (3), **sustulī, sublātum**, to lift, raise, pick up
13 **secūtus est**, he followed
vincula, -ōrum (*n pl*), chains
gravis, -is, -e, heavy
14 **ārea, -ae** (*f*), courtyard
ēvānēscō, ēvānēscere (3), **ēvānuī**, to disappear
15 **dēsertus, -a, -um**, left alone
herba, -ae (*f*), grass, weed
folium, -ī (*n*), leaf
locus, -ī (*m*), place
16 **magistrātūs** (*acc. pl.*), public officials
moneō (2), to warn, advise
ut . . . effoderent, to dig up
17 **implicitus, -a, -um**, wrapped in (+ *abl.*)
pūblicē, publicly
sepulta sunt, were buried

II.

Sed simulācrum suprā Athēnodōrī caput sonābat. Athēnodōrus respexit rūrsus simulacrum, quod iterum manū eum invītābat. Subitō Athēnodōrus lūmen sustulit et simulācrum secūtus est. Ībat illud tardē, quod vincula gravia erant. Postquam simulācrum advēnit in āream domūs, subitō ēvānuit. Athēnodōrus dēsertus herbās et folia in eō locō āreae posuit. Prīmā lūce īvit ad magistrātūs, monuit ut illum locum effoderent. Invēnērunt hominis ossa vinculīs implicita; ossa pūblicē sepulta sunt. Simulācrum numquam iterum domuī appropinquāvit.

Comprehension Questions

8. What made Athenodorus turn and look a second time? (10)
9. What was the ghost doing this time? (11–12)
10. What did Athenodorus do? (12–13)
11. Why did the ghost move slowly? (13)
12. At what location did the ghost vanish? (14)
13. How did Athenodorus mark the spot? (15)
14. What did Athenodorus do the next morning? (16)
15. What was found in the courtyard of the house? (17)
16. Why did the ghost never appear again? (17–18)

THE PASSAGE AS A WHOLE FOR DISCUSSION AND A PROJECT

I.

Ubi coepit advesperāscere, Athēnodōrus iussit servōs lectum movēre in prīmam domūs partem. Tum servōs dīmīsit. Ipse epistulam scrībere coepit, quod dē simulācrīs cōgitāre nōlēbat. Prīmum erat silentium noctis. Deinde audīvit ferrum et vincula sonantia. Ille oculōs nōn sustulit sed animum offirmāvit et scrībere perrēxit. Tum fragor crēbuit et appropinquāvit. Athēnodōrus respexit, vīdit et agnōvit simulācrum, quod quiētē stābat et manū invītābat Athēnodōrum. Ille tamen nōn īvit sed revēnit ad epistulam, nōn timēns simulācrum.

II.

Sed simulācrum suprā Athēnodōrī caput sonābat. Athēnodōrus respexit rūrsus simulacrum, quod iterum manū eum invītābat. Subitō Athēnodōrus lūmen sustulit et simulācrum secūtus est. Ībat illud tardē, quod vincula gravia erant. Postquam simulācrum advēnit in āream domūs, subitō ēvānuit. Athēnodōrus dēsertus herbās et folia in eō locō āreae posuit. Prīmā lūce īvit ad magistrātūs, monuit ut illum locum effoderent. Invēnērunt hominis ossa vinculīs implicita; ossa pūblicē sepulta sunt. Simulācrum numquam iterum domuī appropinquāvit.

Discussion

Do you find the three ghost stories in Pliny's letter convincing? If so, how and why? If not, why not?

Project

At the end of the letter Pliny asks his friend Licinius Sura to give the question of whether or not ghosts exist his most serious consideration. Pliny wants a reply from his friend that will be worthy of his friend's extensive education and vast learning. He suggests that Licinius might argue both sides of the question, but he urges that he come down firmly on one side or the other so that Pliny will not be left in suspense, uncertainty, and doubt.

Pretend you are Licinius Sura and write in English a reply to Pliny's letter.

10
THE AQUEDUCTS OF ANCIENT ROME

Pliny the Elder, *Natural History* XXXVI.121–123

(after Chapter 22)

INTRODUCTION

Pliny the Elder (the uncle of Pliny the Younger, whose letters you have read in this book) lived from A.D. 23 to 79 and was educated in Rome. His military service began with the armies on the Rhine. During Nero's reign (A.D. 54–68) he returned to Italy to pursue rhetorical and grammatical studies. During the reign of Vespasian (A.D. 69–79), Pliny began to write a 37-book encyclopedia entitled *Natural History* (*Naturalis historia*), which he completed by A.D. 77. He died in 79, when he was commander of the fleet at Misenum on the Bay of Naples and attempted to rescue survivors of the eruption of Mt. Vesuvius. Of his many works, only the *Natural History* survives.

In Book 36 of the *Natural History*, Pliny discusses the system that supplied water for the city of Rome. In the passage presented here, Pliny gives a brief history of the aqueducts and discusses their contribution to the quality of life of the Romans. He concludes that the construction of aqueducts to meet Rome's growing need for water was an unparalleled achievement for mankind and, in addition, an advancement for civilization.

The pictures in this chapter illustrate the building of aqueducts and the engineering know-how of the Romans.

The first step in construction was to draw a profile of the site chosen. The first picture (top of page 67) shows workmen using the chorobate, a leveling instrument, to accomplish this. It enabled surveyors to create an imaginary horizontal line over the entire route of the aqueduct (middle of page 67). The aqueduct was built on a gradual slope to keep the water moving. Not until the Aqua Traiana, built in A.D. 109, was a water pump used on an aqueduct.

The earliest aqueducts, the Aqua Appia (built in 312 B.C.) and the Anio Vetus (built in 272 B.C.), consisted of tunnels driven through the hills. The Anio Vetus, however, needed a few short bridges for the water conduit to cross narrow valleys and ravines. The Aqua Marcia (144 B.C.) was the first aqueduct to use arches on a large scale. The next illustration (bottom of page 67) demonstrates these arches. Vertical piers rest on foundations sunk deep into the ground, and over the piers a conduit of water (the aqueduct itself) was carried on a row of arches. When a hill obstructed the path of an aqueduct, the workers dug a tunnel through it and lined the tunnel with stone. The last picture (page 69) illustrates this.

Maintenance of the aqueducts was an ongoing task, and in 33 B.C. the aedile Agrippa was put in charge of the aqueducts and was responsible for their upkeep until his death in 12 B.C. In the following year the Emperor Augustus founded a permanent board known as the **cūrātōrēs aquārum**. In A.D. 97, Sextus Iunius Frontinus was appointed by the Emperor Nerva as the "caretaker of the water supply." As **cūrātor aquārum**, Frontinus began writing *De aquis urbis Romae*, a two-volume account of the nine aqueducts of Rome. In this work he elaborated upon the many problems that he faced in carrying out his duties as caretaker of the water supply. Maintenance, water pollution, and political and fiscal corruption are just a few of the problems Frontinus had to deal with. He also discussed the many ways in which the city benefited from the efficient running of the aqueducts:

> The appearance of the city is cleaner, the air is purer, and the causes have been removed of the rather unhealthy atmosphere, which gave the air of the city so bad a reputation with the ancients.
>
> (*De aquis urbis*, II.88)

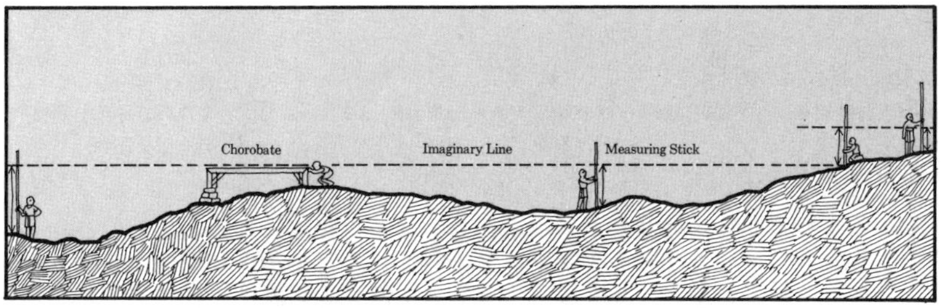

Drawing a profile of the site

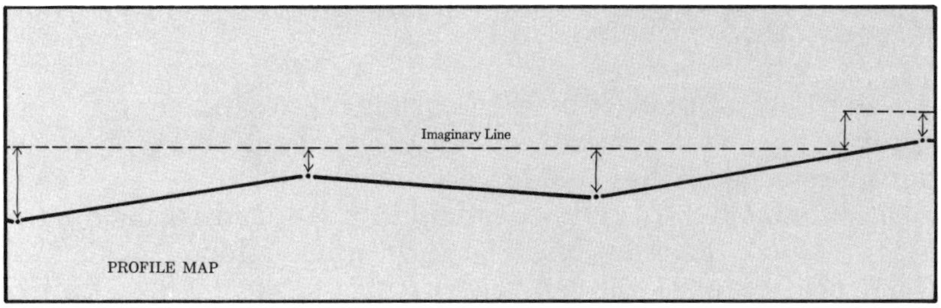

Creating an imaginary horizontal line

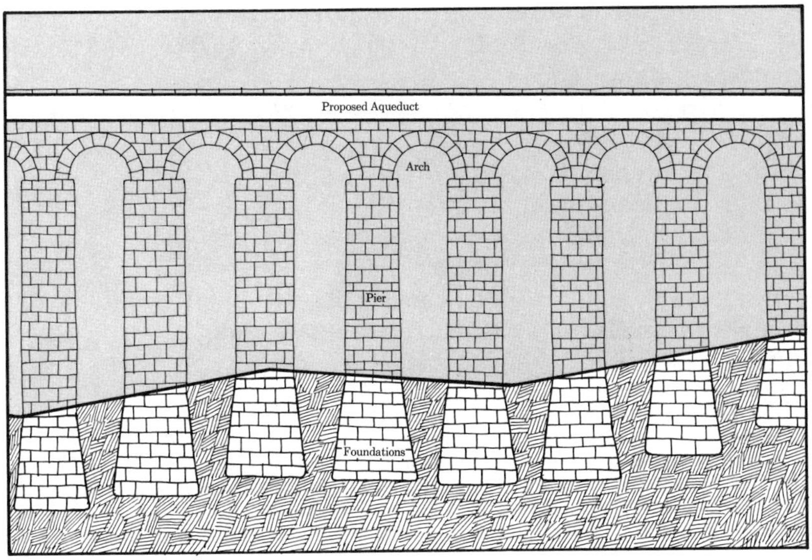

Construction of arches

1 **senātus**, senate
Q. (Quīntus) Marcius Rēx, praetor of 144 B.C. Praetors were Roman magistrates who helped the consuls administer justice, command armies, and carry out other tasks as described in this passage.
ductūs aquārum, aqueducts
Appius, -a, -um, named for Appius (i.e., Appius Claudius Caecus, poet, censor in 312, and consul in 307 and 296 B.C.). The **Aqua Appia** was the first aqueduct built to bring water to Rome.
2 **Aniēnis, -is, -e**, of the Anio river (a tributary of the Tiber). The **Aniō Vetus** was built in 272 B.C. and brought water from the Anio to Rome. (**Vetus** means "old," and the name **Aniō Vetus** was given to the aqueduct after the building of another aqueduct called the **Aniō Novus** in A.D. 52).
Tepulus, -a, -um, Tepulan. The **Aqua Tepula**, built about 125 B.C., brought water to Rome from the Alban hills.
reficiō, reficere (3), **refēcī, refectum**, to restore, repair
cuniculus, -ī (*m*), rabbit, subterranean passage, tunnel
mōns, montis (*m*), mountain, hill
novus, -a, -um, new
3 **aqua, -ae** (*f*), water (here it means "aqueduct")
appellātus, -a, -um, called, named. The **Aqua Marcia** was the first aqueduct to use arches on a large scale.
addūcō, addūcere (3), **addūxī, adductum**, to lead on, bring
4 **praetūra, -ae** (*f*), the office of the praetor, praetorship
cōnficiō, cōnficere (3), **cōnfēcī, cōnfectum**, to accomplish, finish
Agrippa, -ae (*m*), Marcus Vipsanius Agrippa, friend and supporter of the emperor Augustus, aedile (official in charge of public works) in 33 B.C.
aedīlitās, aedīlitātis (*f*), the office of an aedile at Rome, aedileship
5 **Virgō, Virginis** (*f*), the **Aqua Virgō**, built in 19 B.C. and noted for the coolness of its waters
adiciō, adicere (3), **adiēcī, adiectum**, to add
cēterī, -ae, -a, other
ēmendō (1), to repair
6 **lacūs** (*acc. pl.*), lake, tank, reservoir
praetereā, moreover, furthermore, besides
saliēns, salientis (*m*), fountain
castellum, -ī (*n*), small reservoir or distribution point on an aqueduct
complūrēs, complūrēs, complūra, several, many
7 **magnificē**, magnificently
ōrnātus, -a, -um, furnished, equipped, decorated

PLINY THE ELDER, *NATURAL HISTORY* XXXVI.121–123

I.

Senātus Q. Marcium Rēgem iussit ductūs aquārum Appiae, Aniēnis, Tepulae reficere. Cuniculōs per montēs ēgit, et novam aquam ā nōmine suō appellātam ad urbem addūxit. Intrā praetūrae suae tempus eam cōnfēcit. Agrippa in aedīlitāte Virginem aquam adiēcit, cēterōs ductūs aquārum ēmendāvit, lacūs DCC fēcit, praetereā salientēs D, castella CXXX, complūra magnificē ōrnāta.

Comprehension Questions

1. What did the senate order Q. Marcius Rex to do? (1–2)
2. What two things did Q. Marcius Rex do? (2–3)
3. How did his new aqueduct acquire its name? (3)
4. When did he complete it? (3–4)
5. What two things that Agrippa did are mentioned first? (4–5)
6. How many basins, fountains, and distribution points did he make? (6)
7. In what manner were many of the distribution points decorated? (7)

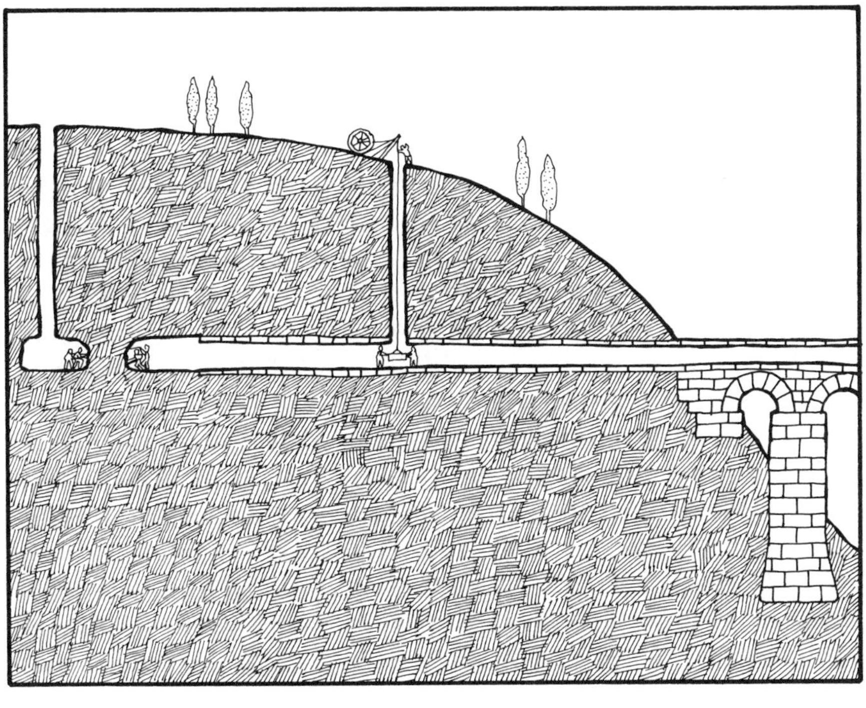

Tunneling a channel for an aqueduct

8 **opus, operis** (*n*), work, public works (such as those involved in the supply of water)
signum, -ī (*n*), mark, sign, (here) sculptured figure, statue
aereus, -a, -um, made of bronze
aut, or
marmoreus, -a, -um, made of marble
impōnō, impōnere (3), **imposuī, impositum**, to place on, put on
9 **columna, -ae** (*f*), column
marmor, marmoris (*n*), marble
annus, -ī (*m*), year
cōnficiō, cōnficere (3), **cōnfēcī, cōnfectum**, to accomplish, finish
10 **ūndēsexāgintā** = **ūnus** + **dē** (from) + **sexāgintā** (60) = 59
ūndēsexāgintā diēbus, on (for) 59 days
lūdī, -ōrum (*m pl*), games (as in the Circus)
grātuītus, -a, -um, costing nothing, free of charge
praebeō, praebēre (2), **praebuī, praebitum**, to offer, present, make available
balneae, -ārum (*f*), public establishment for bathing, baths
11 **Rōmae**, in Rome
īnfīnītus, -a, -um, infinite
augeō, augēre (2), **auxī, auctum**, to increase

II.

Deinde operibus eīs signa CCC aerea aut marmorea imposuit et columnās ē marmore CCCC. Omnia ūnō annō cōnfēcit. Ūndēsexāgintā diēbus lūdōs fēcit et grātuītās praebuit balneās CLXX . Nunc Rōmae ad īnfīnītum numerum balneae auxērunt.

Comprehension Questions

8. What did Agrippa add to his public works? (8–9)
9. How much time did Agrippa take to do all this? (9)
10. How did he celebrate the completion of these works? (10–11)
11. How have things changed since those days? (11)

12 **imperātor, imperātōris** (*m*), emperor
C. Caesar, the emperor Gaius (Caligula), who began the **Aqua Claudia** and the **Aniō Novus** in A.D. 38
ductūs aquārum, aqueducts
coepit, he began
Claudius, the emperor Claudius, who finished the **Aqua Claudia** and the **Aniō Novus** in A.D. 52
13 **cōnficiō, cōnficere** (3), **cōnfēcī, cōnfectum**, to accomplish, finish
hī, these (i.e., **hī ductūs aquārum**)
antecēdō, antecēdere (3), **antecessī** (+ *dat.*), to surpass in size or extent
14 **mōns, montis** (*m*), mountain, hill
lāvērunt, they washed, supplied with water
quis, anyone
aestimō (1), to appraise, estimate the value of
abundantia, -ae (*f*), great amount
15 **pūblicum, -ī** (*n*), public, public places
balneae, -ārum (*f*), public establishment for bathing, baths
piscīna, -ae (*f*), fish pond, pool forming part of a water supply system
eurīpus, -ī (*m*) (Greek loan word), strait, inland channel or waterway, canal
suburbānus, -a, -um, situated close to the city (usually Rome)
16 **spatium, -ī** (*n*), distance
venientis (*gen. sing.*), coming
exstructus, -a, -um, erected
arcūs (*acc. pl.*), arches
perfossus, -a, -um, dug through
17 **convallis, convallis** (*f*), enclosed valley
aequātus, -a, -um, leveled
dīcet nihil . . . esse, he will say nothing to be. . . .
magis, to a greater extent, more
mīrandus, -a, -um, remarkable, wonderful, amazing
tōtus, -a, -um, the whole, all
orbis, orbis (*m*), disc, sphere, globe
18 **terra, -ae** (*f*), land
orbis terrārum, the world

III.

Imperātor C. Caesar aliōs ductūs aquārum coepit. Claudius hōs cōnfēcit. Hī omnibus aliīs antecessērunt et omnēs urbis montēs lāvērunt. Sī quis aestimāverit abundantiam aquārum in pūblicō, balneīs, piscīnīs, eurīpīs, domibus, hortīs, suburbānīs vīllīs, spatia aquae venientis, exstructōs arcūs, montēs perfossōs, convallēs aequātās, dīcet nihil magis mīrandum esse in tōtō orbe terrārum.

Comprehension Questions

12. What did the emperors Gaius Caesar and Claudius do? (12–13)
13. How did these imperial aqueducts compare with the earlier ones? (13)
14. In what ways was the abundant supply of water used? (15–16)
15. What four things are remarkable about the way water was brought to the city? (16–17)
16. How does Pliny evaluate the accomplishment represented by the aqueducts? (17–18)

Ruins of the **Aqua Claudia** near Rome

THE PASSAGE AS A WHOLE FOR DISCUSSION

I.

Senātus Q. Marcium Rēgem iussit ductūs aquārum Appiae, Aniēnis, Tepulae reficere. Cuniculōs per montēs ēgit, et novam aquam ā nōmine suō appellātam ad urbem addūxit. Intrā praetūrae suae tempus eam cōnfēcit. Agrippa in aedīlitāte Virginem aquam adiēcit, cēterōs ductūs aquārum ēmendāvit, lacūs DCC fēcit, praetereā salientēs D, castella CXXX, complūra magnificē ōrnāta.

II.

Deinde operibus eīs signa CCC aerea aut marmorea imposuit et columnās ē marmore CCCC. Omnia ūnō annō cōnfēcit. Ūndēsexāgintā diēbus lūdōs fēcit et grātuītās praebuit balneās CLXX . Nunc Rōmae ad īnfīnītum numerum balneae auxērunt.

III.

Imperātor C. Caesar aliōs ductūs aquārum coepit. Claudius hōs cōnfēcit. Hī omnibus aliīs antecessērunt et omnēs urbis montēs lavērunt. Sī quis aestimāverit abundantiam aquārum in pūblicō, balneīs, piscīnīs, eurīpīs, domibus, hortīs, suburbānīs vīllīs, spatia aquae venientis, exstructōs arcūs, montēs perfossōs, convallēs aequātās, dīcet nihil magis mīrandum esse in tōtō orbe terrārum.

Discussion Questions

1. What benefits did an expanded water supply bring to the quality of private and public life in the city?
2. Why do you think Agrippa would add such magnificent decorations to the water supply? (6–7)
3. What political purpose would be served by the public games and free baths? (10–11)
4. What was the major benefit of the aqueducts constructed by Gaius Caesar and Claudius? (14–15)
5. Frontinus states: "With such a multitude of indispensable structures carrying so many aqueducts, you may compare the idle pyramids or the useless, though celebrated, works of the Greeks!" (*De aquis urbis Romae* I.16) How did the architectural and engineering skills required by the aqueducts reflect the talents and character of the Romans as opposed to those of the Egyptians or the Greeks?

11
FINDING ONE'S WAY IN ANCIENT ROME

Terence, *The Brothers* 571–584

(after "Rome," Book 2, pages 72–75)

INTRODUCTION

How did the Romans know where to deliver something or where to find a person they wished to visit? Today this is quite easy: we simply find the name of the street and the number of the house. However, many streets in Rome had no names and houses had no numbers, so the Romans had no addresses in our sense of the term.

In the country or in a small town, there was no problem. To find the house you were looking for, you simply asked the first person you met for directions. In Rome and other large cities, however, finding a specific home might involve a great deal of labor and luck. It was easy to locate the homes of public figures, for everyone knew where they lived. People could also use their homes as points of reference.

Other points of reference might include statues, columns, temples, and public buildings, such as granaries, barracks, and colonnades, as well as sacred groves, gardens, and trees. Sometimes a landmark became so familiar that its name was given to a street or whole district. For instance, even today Rome has the Street of the Marble Foot, so named because the remains of a colossal statue, a large foot, are found at its entrance. Streets were also often named after the type of shop found in them.

In the following scene from a play by Terence, a slave named Syrus is directing Demea to a specific house near which he will find his brother, for whom he is looking. The passage gives us an idea of how complicated it could be to give and receive directions in ancient times.

1 **illīus**, of that
locus, -ī (*m*), place
2 **sit**, (he) is
3 **ergō**, so, therefore
4 **porticus, -ūs** (*f*), covered walk having its roof supported by columns, portico, colonnade
apud (+ *acc.*), at, near
macellum, -ī (*n*), market
hāc (*adverb*), by this route, this way
deorsum (*adverb*), downward, down
5 **eam**, that
6 **praetereō, praeterīre** (*irreg.*), **praeteriī, praeteritum**, to pass by, go past
rēctus, -a, -um, direct, straight
platea, -ae (*f*), street
  hāc rēctā plateā, straight along this street
sūrsum (*adverb*), upward, up
vēneris, you will have come
7 **clīvus, -ī** (*m*), slope
versum (*adverb*), turned, turning (here emphasizes **deorsum**)
posteā, next
8 **hanc**, this
sacellum, -ī (*n*), small shrine
angiportum, -ī (*n*), narrow passage, alley, lane
propter (*adverb*), nearby
11 **illī** (*adverb*), at that place, there
caprifīcus, -ī (*f*), wild fig-tree

TERENCE, *THE BROTHERS* 571–584

I.

SYRUS: At nōmen nesciō illīus hominis, sed locum sciō ubi sit.

DĒMEA: Dīc ergō locum.

SYRUS: Scīsne porticum apud macellum hāc deorsum?

DĒMEA: Certē eam porticum sciō.

SYRUS: Praeterī hāc rēctā plateā sūrsum: ubi eō vēneris, clīvus deorsum versum est: hāc tē praecipitā. Posteā est ad hanc manum sacellum: ibi angiportum propter est.

DĒMEA: Ubi?

SYRUS: Illī ubi etiam caprificus magna est.

DĒMEA: Sciō.

Comprehension Questions

1. What doesn't Syrus know? (1) What does he know? (1–2)
2. What is the **porticus** near? (4)
3. In what direction must Demea go to arrive at the **clīvus**? (6–7)
4. What will Demea come to next? (8)
5. What is beside the **sacellum**? (8–9)
6. What is the next landmark? (11)

13 **hāc** (*adverb*), by this route, this way
pergō, pergere (3), **perrēxī, perrēctum**, to move onward, proceed
14 **quidem**, indeed, but
angiportum, -ī (*n*), narrow passage, alley, lane
pervius, -a, -um, passable
15 **vērus, -a, -um**, true
hercle, by Hercules!
vāh, oh!
errō (1), to make a mistake
mē hominem esse, that I am a man
16 **porticus, -ūs** (*f*), covered walk having its roof supported by columns, portico, colonnade
rūrsus (*adverb*), again
sānē (*adverb*), certainly
multō, by much, much
celerius, more quickly, faster
17 **minor, minoris**, smaller, less
errātiō, errātiōnis (*f*), wandering about
dīves, dīvitis, rich
19 **praeterieris**, you will have gone past
sinistra, -ae (*f*), left-hand side
hāc rēctā plateā, straight along this street
20 **Diāna, -ae** (*f*), goddess of hunting
dextra, -ae (*f*), right-hand side
21 **priusquam**, before
apud (+ *acc.*), at, near
lacus, -ūs (*m*), pond, pool
22 **pistrilla, -ae** (*f*), small bakery
exadversum (*adverb*), on the other side, opposite
fabrica, -ae (*f*), workshop

II.

SYRUS: Hāc perge.

DĒMEA: Id quidem angiportum nōn est pervium.

SYRUS: Vērum, hercle! Vāh, errāvī: scīs mē hominem esse. In porticum rūrsus redī. Sānē hāc multō celerius ībis et minor est errātiō. Scīsne Cratīnī dīvitis domum?

DĒMEA: Sciō.

SYRUS: Ubi eam praeterieris, ī ad sinistram hāc rēctā plateā; ubi ad templum Diānae vēneris, ī ad dextram. Priusquam ad portam veniās, apud ipsum lacum est pistrilla et exadversum est fabrica. Ibi est.

Comprehension Questions

7. Why is the **angiportum** not a good route? (14)
8. To what place does Syrus tell Demea to return? (15–16)
9. What two advantages will the new route have? (16–17)
10. In what direction is Demea supposed to go after he passes Cratinus' house? (19)
11. What building will he approach next? (20)
12. In what direction should he then turn? (20)
13. Where is the **pistrilla**? (21–22)
14. Where will Demea find his brother? (22)

Bread making in a Roman **pistrilla**

THE PASSAGE AS A WHOLE FOR ACTING

The humor of this dialogue can best be appreciated by acting it out. Practice reading the Latin aloud. Add appropriate gestures and gesticulations. Keep in mind that this is a dialogue between a wily and somewhat malicious slave (Syrus) and a stodgy old man (Demea), who is being led on and duped by the slave. Vary the tone and expression of your voice to fit the intentions and feelings of the speakers in each sentence they speak. Do not hesitate to exaggerate for dramatic and comic effect. Choose a partner and perform the dialogue in front of your class.

SYRUS: At nōmen nesciō illīus hominis, sed locum sciō ubi sit.

DĒMEA: Dīc ergō locum.

SYRUS: Scīsne porticum apud macellum hāc deorsum?

DĒMEA: Certē eam porticum sciō.

SYRUS: Praeterī hāc rēctā plateā sūrsum: ubi eō vēneris, clīvus deorsum versum est: hāc tē praecipitā. Posteā est ad hanc manum sacellum: ibi angiportum propter est.

DĒMEA: Ubi?

SYRUS: Illī ubi etiam caprifīcus magna est.

DĒMEA: Sciō.

SYRUS: Hāc perge.

DĒMEA: Id quidem angiportum nōn est pervium.

SYRUS: Vērum, hercle! Vāh, errāvī: scīs mē hominem esse. In porticum rūrsus redī. Sānē hāc multō celerius ībis et minor est errātiō. Scīsne Cratīnī dīvitis domum?

DĒMEA: Sciō.

SYRUS: Ubi eam praeterieris, ī ad sinistram hāc rēctā plateā; ubi ad templum Diānae vēneris, ī ad dextram. Priusquam ad portam veniās, apud ipsum lacum est pistrilla et exadversum est fabrica. Ibi est.

How would you find your way in this ancient Roman town?

12
DOMUS AUREA NERONIS
THE GOLDEN HOUSE OF NERO

Suetonius, *Life of Nero* XXXI.1–2

(after "Eucleides the Statistician," Book 2, pages 77–79)

INTRODUCTION

Nero, the fifth Roman emperor, ruled from A.D. 54 until he died in A.D. 68 at the age of 30. He was an extravagant monarch, who inspired either strong hatred or devotion in his subjects. His excesses became proverbial, and they were fully described by Romans during and after his reign.

Since Nero loved the Greeks and their culture, he traveled throughout the Greek world to participate in athletic and dramatic contests. During the great fire of Rome in A.D. 64, he is said to have stood on the roof of his palace in the attire of a Greek tragic actor and played his lyre while singing of the fall of Troy.

The Roman historian Tacitus was alive at the time, and he later described the great fire:

> Destruction followed. Some said it was an accident; others claimed it was set by the emperor. Either way it was more horrible and destructive than any fire before it. The flames sped ahead of all attempts to block them, feeding on the narrow streets, which wound this way and that in irregular patterns. There were panicking women, children, and elderly; some looking out for themselves, some taking care of others; some carrying invalids, some waiting for them; some delaying, some hurrying. Confusion reigned.
>
> No one dared fight the fire because of repeated threats of many who warned them not to. Some were even hurling torches and shouting that they had been ordered to do so. They may have been ordered, or they may have wanted to loot more freely.
>
> (*Annals* XV.38)

Faced with the widespread destruction left by the great fire, Nero undertook a massive building campaign. Most of his energy went toward building a palace for himself. A palace that he had just finished building had been destroyed in the fire. He and his architects remodeled it on a monumental scale. This huge new palace was called the Golden House (**Domus Aurea**).

Tacitus wrote as follows about what Nero did after the great fire:

> Nero put the destruction of the fatherland to good use; he built a house. The gems and gold were not so wonderful; they were old hat and had become commonplace with luxury. The real wonders were the fields and lakes and the "away-from-it-all" effect created by the forests and open spaces with views.
>
> (*Annals* XV.42)

Martial, a Roman poet who was in his middle twenties at the time the Golden House was built, wrote the following poem to the new emperor, Titus (A.D. 79–81). In it he describes how Nero's successors increased their popularity by converting parts of Nero's palace into a park and facilities for the public. Note especially the language with which he speaks of Nero:

> Here where the heavenly Colossus sees the stars close up and high scaffolding rises in the middle way stretched the hated halls of the savage king. There then stood but a single house in the whole city. Here where the venerable structure of this remarkable amphitheater is erected was Nero's lake. Here where we marvel at the baths, a swiftly-built gift, his proud estate had snatched houses from the poor. Here where the colonnade of Claudius spreads its shade lay the furthest part of the unfinished palace. Rome is now returned to herself, and under your rule, Titus, the people delight in what used to belong to their master.
>
> (*On the Spectacles* 2)

Discussion Questions

1. What impresses Tacitus most about the Golden House?
2 Why is Tacitus not impressed by its other features?
3. How does Martial refer to Nero?
4. How does he refer to the Golden House?
5 What does he say about Nero's attitude toward his neighbors?
6. How does he describe the Flavian amphitheater?
7. How does he describe the Baths of Titus?
8. What attitude do these writers have toward Nero?
9. What do they think of his conduct in building the Golden House?

1 **damnōsissimus, -a, -um**, most ruinous, spendthrift, extravagant
in aedificandō, in constructing buildings
2 **usque**, all the way
Esquiliae, -ārum (*f pl*), the Esquiline Hill
nōminō (1), to name
vestibulum, -ī (*n*), entrance hall
3 **colossus, -ī** (*m*), large statue
effigiēs, -ēī (*f*), likeness
  ipsīus effigiē, in likeness of himself
laxitās, laxitātis (*f*), spaciousness, expanse
4 **porticus, -ūs** (*f*), portico, covered walkway
triplex, triplicis, triple
mīliārius, -a, -um, one mile long
stagnum, -ī (*n*), pond
mare, maris (*n*), sea
5 **īnstar** (+ *preceding gen.*), like
circumsaeptus, -a, -um, closed in, surrounded
speciēs, -ēī (*f*), appearance, likeness
6 **īnsuper** (*adverb*), in addition
pascua, -ae (*f*), pasturage
7 **genus, generis** (*n*), kind
pecus, pecudis (*f*), livestock, domesticated animals
fera, -ae (*f*), wild animal

SUETONIUS, *LIFE OF NERO* XXXI.1–2

Suetonius, a Roman biographer who was born the year after Nero died, described Nero's building of the Golden House in some detail. After speaking at great length of Nero's lust, extravagance, avarice, and cruelty, he went on to report as follows:

I.

Damnōsissimus tamen erat in aedificandō. Domum ā Palātīnō usque ad Esquiliās fēcit, quam auream nōmināvit. In vestibulō colossus CXX pedum stābat ipsīus effigiē. Laxitās vestibulī erat maxima: porticūs triplicēs mīliāriās habēbat. Stagnum maris īnstar aderat, circumsaeptum aedificiīs ad urbium speciem; īnsuper aderant agrī atque vīneae et pascua silvaeque, cum multitūdine omnis generis pecudum ac ferārum.

Comprehension Questions

1. How was Nero especially extravagant? (1)
2. Where did Nero build the **Domus Aurea**? (1–2)
3. What three things does Suetonius tell us about the colossal statue? (2–3)
4. Describe the entrance hall. (3–4) How many rows of columns did its porticos have? How long were the colonnades?
5. What did the pond resemble? (4–5)
6. What did the buildings around it resemble? (5)
7. What other four things were present? (6)
8. What kind of livestock and wild animals were kept in the pastures and woods? (7)

Nero's Golden House, as imagined by a modern artist

8 **litus, -a, -um**, overlaid
distinctus, -a, -um, set off, decorated
gemma, -ae (*f*), gem
cēnātiō, cēnātiōnis (*f*), dining room
9 **laqueāre, laqueāris** (*n*), paneled ceiling
tabula, -ae (*f*), plank, panel
eburneus, -a, -um, made of ivory
versātilis, -is, -e, capable of being turned around, revolving
10 **flōs, flōris** (*m*), flower
unguentum, -ī (*n*), ointment, perfume
spargēbantur, were sprinkled
balneae, -ārum (*f pl*), baths
marīnus, -a, -um, of the sea
albulus, -a, -um, sulfurous
11 **dēdicō** (1), to dedicate
12 **quasi**, as if, like
coepī, I have begun

II.

In domō omnia aurō lita, distincta gemmīs erant. Cēnātiōnēs laqueāria cum tabulīs eburneīs versātilibus habēbant. Ex eīs flōrēs atque unguenta spargēbantur. Balneae marīnās et albulās aquās habēbant. Hanc domum ubi dēdicāvit, "Ego tandem," inquit, "quasi homō habitāre coepī."

Comprehension Questions

9. With what two things was everything in the house decorated? (8)
10. Of what material were the ceiling panels in the dining room made? (9)
11. What unique capability did they have? (9)
12. What did they sprinkle on the dinner guests? (10)
13. What two kinds of water did the baths have? (10–11)
14. In what manner did Nero claim he was able to live after the house was finished? (11–12)

Inside Nero's Golden House

THE PASSAGE AS A WHOLE FOR DISCUSSION

I.

Damnōsissimus tamen erat in aedificandō. Domum ā Palātīnō usque ad Esquiliās fēcit, quam auream nōmināvit. In vestibulō colossus CXX pedum stābat ipsīus effigiē. Laxitās vestibulī erat maxima: porticūs triplicēs mīliāriās habēbat. Stagnum maris īnstar aderat, circumsaeptum aedificiīs ad urbium speciem; īnsuper aderant agrī atque vīneae et pascua silvaeque, cum multitūdine omnis generis pecudum ac ferārum.

II.

In domō omnia aurō lita, distincta gemmīs erant. Cēnātiōnēs laqueāria cum tabulīs eburneīs versātilibus habēbant. Ex eīs flōrēs atque unguenta spargēbantur. Balneae marīnās et albulās aquās habēbant. Hanc domum ubi dēdicāvit, "Ego tandem," inquit, "quasi homō habitāre coepī."

Discussion Questions

1. What were the unique features of the **Domus Aurea** in terms of size, novelty, luxury, extravagance, and imagination?
2. Why do you think Nero included these unique features in his house? (For help in answering this question you may want to reread the passage from Tacitus quoted at the top of page 83.)
3. What is the point of making part of the house look like a city, part like cultivated rural land, and part like the wild forest?
4. Is it possible that *everything* was **aurō lita** and **distincta gemmīs** (8)? What kind of a statement is Suetonius making here? What is his purpose?
5. What does Nero mean by his words quoted in lines 11–12?
6. What impression do his words leave in your mind?
7. Compare Nero's **Domus Aurea** to Pliny's Laurentine villa and Horace's Sabine farm as described in Chapters 3 and 4 of this book.

13
FINDING A DATE IN ANCIENT ROME OR WHY SOME MEN WENT TO THE CHARIOT RACES

Ovid, *The Art of Love* I.135–162

(after Chapter 26)

INTRODUCTION

Publius Ovidius Naso, now commonly known as Ovid, was a leading poet of Rome by A.D. 8. He was a younger contemporary of Horace and Vergil, other poets of the Golden Age of Latin literature. Ovid, however, unlike Horace and Vergil, did not receive the patronage of the emperor Augustus and did not support Augustus' policies in his writings. Augustus exiled Ovid in A.D. 8 to Tomis, a town on the Black Sea. Tomis was on the extreme edge of the Roman Empire, and few people there spoke or read Latin. Ovid was never allowed to return to Rome.

While Ovid was at Tomis, he wrote a series of poems called *Unhappy Things* (*Tristia*), in which he gives the reasons for his exile: **carmen et error** ("a poem and a mistake"). The **error** was something he did that offended Augustus personally. The **carmen** was presumably his poem entitled *The Art of Love* (*Ars amatoria*). Ovid addressed Book II of *Unhappy Things* to Augustus, and in it he wrote an elaborate defense of *The Art of Love*. This plea was of no avail.

The Art of Love is a poem in which Ovid teaches men how to find a girlfriend (Book I) and how to keep her (Book II). Book III, which gives parallel instructions to women, was added later at their request. In Book I, Ovid lists several places in Rome where one can meet women: monuments, the theater, the chariot races, and triumphal processions. However, since marriages in respectable Roman society were arranged by parents, we might question what sort of women Ovid is describing in this poem and what sort of relationship men would have with them.

The action in the following passage takes place at the chariot races in the Circus Maximus.

1 **certāmen, certāminis** (*n*), competition, sporting contest
nōbilis, -is, -e, noble, famous
commodum, -ī (*n*), advantage, opportunity
2 **capāx** (+ *gen.*), holding a lot (of)
populus, -ī (*m*), people
proximus ā dominā, right next to a lady
  domina, -ae (*f*), mistress, lady of the house, (here) object of attention, loved one
3 **prohibeō, prohibēre** (2), **prohibuī, prohibitum**, to keep apart, prevent
iungō, iungere (3), **iūnxī, iūnctum**, to join, put next to
latus, lateris (*n*), side
quā . . . usque, as close as
cuius, whose?
4 **studiōsē**, actively, eagerly
mora, -ae (*f*), delay
cuicui favet illa, whomever she favors
5 **utque**, and as
fit, it happens
gremium, -ī (*n*), lap, bosom
pulvis, pulveris (*m*), dust
forte, by chance
dēcidō, dēcidere (3), **dēcidī**, to fall down
digitus, -ī (*m*), finger
6 **excutiō, excutere** (3), **excussī, excussum**, to shake out, brush off
etsī, even if
quaelibet causa, any excuse
7 **sit**, let (it) be
aptus, -a, -um (+ *dat.*), suitable (for), useful (to)
officium, -ī (*n*), helpful or beneficial act, service
parva, little things
levis, -is, -e, light in weight, carefree
capiō, capere (3), **cēpī, captum**, to seize
8 **ūtilis, -is, -e** (+ *dat.*), useful (to)
pulvīnus, -ī (*m*), cushion
compōnō, compōnere (3), **composuī, compositum**, to place together, arrange, adjust
facilī manū, with a skillful hand
prōdest = est ūtile
9 **ventus, -ī** (*m*), wind
tenuis, -is, -e, thin
tabella, -ae (*f*), tablet
  tenuī tabellā, with a thin tablet (which served as a program)
scamna, -ōrum (*n pl*), stool
tener, tenera, tenerum, soft, tender, delicate

OVID, *THE ART OF LOVE* I.135–162

Tū pete etiam certāmen equōrum nōbilium; multa commoda capāx populī Circus habet. Proximus ā dominā sedē; nēmō prohibet. Iunge latus tuum laterī eius quā potes usque. "Cuius equī veniunt?" studiōsē rogā et sine morā favē cuicui favet illa. Utque fit, in gremium puellae pulvis sī forte dēciderit, digitīs eum excute. Etsī nūllus est pulvis, tamen excute nūllum; quaelibet causa sit apta officiō tuō. Parva animōs levēs puellārum capiunt: est ūtile multīs virīs pulvīnum compōnere facilī manū; et prōdest ventōs movēre tenuī tabellā et scamna dare sub tenerum pedem puellae.

Comprehension Questions

1. Where does Ovid suggest a Roman should go to find a date? Why? (1–2)
2. How closely should the man sit to the girl he wants to meet? (2)
3. What physical contact does Ovid recommend? (3)
4. Whose horses should the man favor? (3–4)
5. If dust falls on the girl's lap, what should the man do? (5–6)
6. What should the man do if no dust falls on the girl? (6)
7. What Latin word describes the minds of girls? (7)
8. What three final suggestions does Ovid give for gaining the girl's attention? (8–10)

The chariot races

THE PASSAGE AS A WHOLE FOR DISCUSSION

Tū pete etiam certāmen equōrum nōbilium; multa commoda capāx populī Circus habet. Proximus ā dominā sedē; nēmō prohibet. Iunge latus tuum laterī eius quā potes usque. "Cuius equī veniunt?" studiōsē rogā et sine morā favē cuicui favet illa. Utque fit, in gremium puellae pulvis sī forte dēciderit, digitīs eum excute. Etsī nūllus est pulvis, tamen excute nūllum; quaelibet causa sit apta officiō tuō. Parva animōs levēs puellārum capiunt: est ūtile multīs virīs pulvīnum compōnere facilī manū; et prōdest ventōs movēre tenuī tabellā et scamna dare sub tenerum pedem puellae.

Discussion Questions

1. What form of the verb is frequently used in this passage to convey the speaker's instructions to the would-be lover?
2. Is it easy or difficult to find a girl in the Circus Maximus? Find Latin phrases in the passage to support your answer.
3. a. What attitude does Ovid reveal toward women?
   b. How does he suggest they should be treated?
   c. For what purpose should men treat them in this way?
4. a. What attitude does Ovid reveal toward men?
   b. What does he assume that men want?
   c. How does he urge that they behave in order to get it?
5. a. How does Ovid's description of meeting a woman compare with the ancient Roman practice of arranged marriages?
   b. How does it compare with our own practices of courtship today?
6. What might Augustus have found offensive about this passage?
7. What, if anything, does this passage tell us about a typical Roman's attitude toward the races in the Circus Maximus?

14
PLINY'S VIEWS ON THE CHARIOT RACES

Pliny, *Letters* IX.6

(after Chapter 26)

INTRODUCTION

For Pliny and his *Letters*, see Chapter 3, "Pliny's Laurentine Villa," Chapter 5, "Slaves and Masters in Ancient Rome," and Chapter 9, "Ghosts." Although Pliny wrote his letters to communicate with specific people on specific occasions, he also had in mind publication of the letters as works of literature to be enjoyed by a wider readership. The letter thus became a literary form that was appreciated for its thoughtful content and elegant prose style. The most famous and extensive collection of letters from the ancient world is that of Cicero (first century B.C.). Cicero did not intend his letters to be published, however, and thus they are candid in content and natural in style. They were published after his death by admirers, and hence a trend was started.

Some members of Roman society looked askance at the shameless behavior and self-indulgence typical of many of their compatriots in the imperial period. This letter of Pliny reflects such an attitude and gives his views on what he sees as the Romans' mad passion for the chariot races.

The chariot races, known as the **lūdī circēnsēs**, were among the most popular spectacles in ancient Rome. They were held in the Circus Maximus and were paid for either by the aediles, officers in charge of public works and entertainment, who would put on spectacular events to gain popularity and thereby advance their careers, or by the emperor to keep his popularity with the people. The Circus Maximus was a long stadium between the Palatine and Aventine hills, and it held about 200,000 spectators.

The chariots would emerge from starting stalls (**carcerēs**) when the emperor or presiding official dropped a white handkerchief. They then went seven laps around the track, in the center of which was a long barrier-island (**spīna**) with statues and other ornaments on it. At its ends stood turning posts (**mētae**), which the charioteers tried to round as closely as possible. Then, as now, there was a tremendous amount of betting. People would bet for one of four colors worn by the charioteers: red, white, blue, or green. These colors showed to which of four teams (**factiōnēs**) the charioteer belonged.

1 **C. PLĪNIUS CALVĪSIŌ SUŌ S.**: a form of salutation for beginning a letter. The abbreviation **S.** is for **SALŪTEM** ("greetings") and **DĪCIT** is understood after this. Thus: "Gaius Plinius to Calvisius his [friend] greetings says." Calvisius was a friend of Pliny's from his native Comum in northern Italy.

2 **quiētē**, quietly, peacefully
ac, and
quemadmodum, how? in what way?

3 **nē . . . quidem**, not even

4 **levissimē**, very lightly, slightly
varius, -a, -um, different, varied

5 **semel**, once
ergō, so, therefore
magis, more
mīror, I am amazed, wonder at
tot mīlia virōrum, so many thousands of grown-up men
tam, so

6 **puerīliter**, boyishly, childishly
identidem, again and again, repeatedly
cupiō, cupere (3), **cupīvī, cupītum**, to desire, want
currentēs, running
īnsistentēs (+ *dat.*), standing (on or in)

7 **currus, -ūs** (*m*), chariot

PLINY, *LETTERS* IX.6

I.

C. PLĪNIUS CALVĪSIŌ SUŌ S.

Omne hoc tempus quiētē legō ac scrībō. "Quemadmodum," inquis, "in urbe potes?" Circēnsēs sunt in urbe, quī mē nē levissimē quidem tenent. Nihil novum, nihil varium; satis est semel illōs spectāre. Ergō magis mīror tot mīlia virōrum tam puerīliter identidem cupere currentēs equōs et īnsistentēs curribus hominēs vidēre.

Comprehension Questions

1. What has Pliny been doing? (2)
2. How has he been doing it? (2)
3 Where has he been doing it? (3)
4. Who is asking the question in lines 2–3?
5 Why has Pliny not been at the races instead? (3–4)
6. What three reasons does Pliny give for not attending the races? (4–5)
7. What two things is Pliny amazed that the spectators desire to see? (5–7)
8. With what adverb does Pliny describe the spectators' desire to see the races? (6)

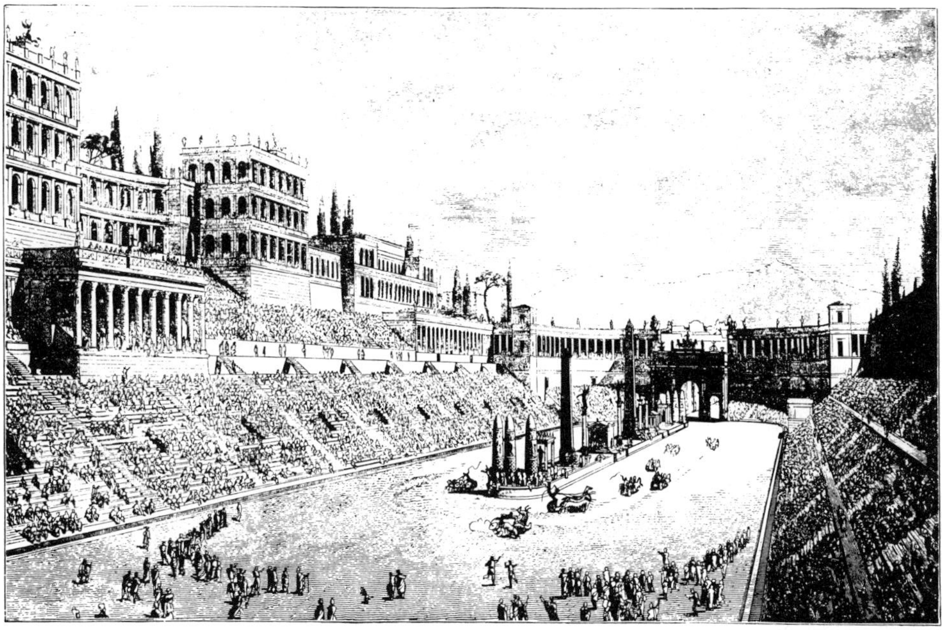

A modern drawing of the Circus Maximus

8 **vēlōcitās, vēlōcitātis** (*f*), swiftness, speed
aut, or
ars, artis (*f*), skill
trahō, trahere (3), **traxī, tractum**, to drag, pull, attract
ratiō, ratiōnis (*f*), reason, justification
nōn nūlla, not none = some
9 **pannus, -ī** (*m*), tunic worn by the charioteer with the color of his faction to distinguish him from the other racers
color, colōris (*m*), color
10 **trānsferō, trānsferre** (*irreg.*), **trānstulī, trānslātum**, to change, exchange
studium, -ī (*n*), enthusiasm
favor, favōris (*m*), favor
transeō, transīre (*irreg.*), **trānsiī, trānsitum**, to cross over, change
11 **grātia, -ae** (*f*), esteem, regard, attraction
auctōritās, auctōritātis (*f*), prestige, authority
vīlissimā, very cheap
mittō, mittere (3), **mīsī, missum**, to send, let go, omit, not mention. Translate freely: "I won't even bother to mention how great are the attraction and authority of one very cheap tunic. . . ."
apud (+ *acc.*), among
12 **vulgus, -ī** (*n*), common people, public
vīlius (*neuter nom. sing.*), cheaper, of less worth
tunicā, than the tunic
gravis, -is, -e, heavy, serious, dignified
13 **capiō, capere** (3), **cēpī, captum**, to take
aliquī, aliqua, aliquod, some, a certain
voluptās, voluptātis (*f*), pleasure
ac, and
14 **libentissimē**, most willingly, with the greatest pleasure
ōtium, -ī (*n*), leisure
litterae, -ārum (*f pl*), letters, literature
collocō (1), to place, put

II.

Sī vēlōcitās equōrum aut ars hominum eōs trahit, est ratiō nōn nūlla; sed nunc favent pannō, pannum amant. Sī equī colōrēs trānsferunt, studium favorque spectātōrum trānsit. Tanta est grātia atque auctōritās in ūnā vīlissimā tunicā, mittō apud vulgus, quod est vīlius tunicā, sed apud quōsdam gravēs hominēs. Capiō aliquam voluptātem, quod haec voluptās mē nōn capit. Ac per hōs diēs libentissimē ōtium meum in litterīs collocō. Valē.

Comprehension Questions

9. What possible explanations does Pliny suggest for the people's eagerness to see the races? (8)
10. What, in fact, is of most interest to the spectators? (9)
11. What would happen if the colors worn by the charioteers were switched? (9–10)
12. What two words in line 11 show what value the *spectators* place on the colored tunics of the charioteers?
13. What word in line 11 shows what value *Pliny* places on the colored tunics of the charioteers?
14. What two groups of people are obsessed with the colored tunics of the charioteers? (11–12)
15. What value does Pliny place on the **vulgus**? (12)
16. From what does Pliny derive pleasure? (13)
17. How does Pliny spend his leisure time? (14)

A charioteer about to round the turning posts at the end of the **spīna**

THE PASSAGE AS A WHOLE FOR DISCUSSION AND DEBATE

I.

C. PLĪNIUS CALVĪSIŌ SUŌ S.

Omne hoc tempus quiētē legō ac scrībō. "Quemadmodum," inquis, "in urbe potes?" Circēnsēs sunt in urbe, quī mē nē levissimē quidem tenent. Nihil novum, nihil varium; satis est semel illōs spectāre. Ergō magis mīror tot mīlia virōrum tam puerīliter identidem cupere currentēs equōs et īnsistentēs curribus hominēs vidēre.

II.

Sī vēlōcitās equōrum aut ars hominum eōs trahit, est ratiō nōn nūlla; sed nunc favent pannō, pannum amant. Sī equī colōrēs trānsferunt, studium favorque spectātōrum trānsit. Tanta est grātia atque auctōritās in ūnā vīlissimā tunicā, mittō apud vulgus, quod est vīlius tunicā, sed apud quōsdam gravēs hominēs. Capiō aliquam voluptātem, quod haec voluptās mē nōn capit. Ac per hōs diēs libentissimē ōtium meum in litterīs collocō. Valē.

Discussion Questions

1. What does this letter tell us about Pliny's likes and dislikes?
2. Do you know people today who share some or all of Pliny's likes and dislikes?
3. What elements of the style of this letter suggest that it was artfully written and intended for publication?
4. How is this letter like or unlike a letter you would write?

Activity

Stage a classroom debate between those who sympathize with Pliny and those who sympathize with the spectators. The debate could be organized as follows. Each student in the class writes down on a sheet of paper one or two arguments in defense of Pliny's views and on another sheet of paper one or two arguments in defense of the spectators. The class then chooses a spokesperson for each side. After reading the written arguments for their respective sides, these two students then conduct a debate in front of the class.

VOCABULARY

A

ā or **ab** (+ *abl.*)	by, from, away from
abeō, abīre (*irreg.*), **abiī, abitum**	to go away
ad (+ *acc.*)	to, toward, at, near
adsum, adesse (*irreg.*), **adfuī**	to be present, near
adveniō, advenīre (4), **advēnī, adventum**	to come to, reach, arrive at
advesperāscit, advesperāscere (3), **advesperāvit**	it is getting dark
aedificium, -ī (*n*)	building
ager, agrī (*m*)	field, territory, land
agnōscō, agnōscere (3), **agnōvī, agnitum**	to recognize
agō, agere (3), **ēgī, āctum**	to do, drive, discuss, debate
alius, alia, aliud	other, another, different
alius . . . alius	one . . . another
alter, altera, alterum	the one, the other (of two), the second
amīcus, -ī (*m*)	friend
amō (1)	to like, love
animus, -ī (*m*)	mind, spirit, will
appropinquō (1) (+ *dat.*)	to approach, draw near to
aqua, -ae (*f*)	water
ārea, -ae (*f*)	open space, threshing-floor, courtyard
at	but
ātrium, -ī (*n*)	atrium, main room
audiō (4)	to hear, listen to
aureus, -a, -um	golden
aurum, -ī (*n*)	gold

B

bonus, -a, -um	good
brevī tempore	in a short time

C

cantō (1)	to sing
caupō, caupōnis (*m*)	innkeeper
cēnō (1)	to dine, eat dinner
certē	certainly, at least
circēnsis, -is, -e	in the circus
clāmō (1)	to shout
clāmor, clāmōris (*m*)	shout, shouting
coepī	I began
cōgitō (1)	to think, consider
cubiculum, -ī (*n*)	bedroom
cubitum īre	to go to bed
cum (+ *abl.*)	with

D

dē (+ *abl.*)	down from, concerning, about
deinde	then, next
dīcō, dīcere (3), **dīxī, dictum**	to say, tell
diēs, -ēī (*m*)	day
diū	for a long time
dō, dare (1), **dedī, datum**	to give
dominus, -ī (*m*)	master, owner
domus, -ūs (*f*)	house, home

E

ego	I
eō, īre (*irreg.*), **īvī, itum**	to go
eō (*adverb*)	there, to that place
epistula, -ae (*f*)	letter
equus, -ī (*m*)	horse
et	and, also
etiam	also, even, still
ex, ē (+ *abl.*)	from, out of

F

faciō, facere (3), **fēcī, factum**	to make, do
faveō, favēre (2), **fāvī, fautum** (+ *dat.*)	to favor, support
ferō, ferre (*irreg.*), **tulī, lātum**	to carry, bring, bear
fragor, fragōris (*m*)	crash, noise, din

H

habeō (2)	to have, hold
habitō (1)	to live, dwell
homō, hominis (*m*)	man, fellow
hortus, -ī (*m*)	garden

I

iam	now, already
ibi	there
igitur	therefore
ille, illa, illud	that, he, she, it
in (+ *abl.*)	in, on, among
in (+ *acc.*)	into, toward, until
inquit	he (she) says, said
intrā (+ *acc.*)	inside, within
intrō (1)	to enter
inveniō, invenīre (4), **invēnī, inventum**	to come upon, find
ipse, ipsa, ipsum	-self
is, ea, id	he, she, it, this, that
iterum	again, a second time
iubeō, iubēre (2), **iussī, iussum**	to order

L

laetus, -a, -um	joyful, happy
lectus, -ī (*m*)	bed, couch

legō, legere (3), **lēgī, lēctum**	to read
lūx, lūcis (*f*)	light

M

magnus, -a, -um	big, large, loud (voice)
manus, -ūs (*f*)	hand, side (when giving directions)
maximus, -a, -um	very great, greatest, very large
meus, -a, -um	my, mine
moveō, movēre (2), **mōvī, mōtum**	to move, shake
multitūdō, multitūdinis (*f*)	crowd
multus, -a, -um	much, (plural) many
mūs, mūris (*m*)	mouse

N

nam	for
-ne	(indicates a question)
nēmō, nēminis (*m*)	no one
nesciō (4)	to be ignorant, not know
nihil	nothing
nōlō, nōlle (*irreg.*), **nōluī**	to be unwilling, not wish, refuse
nōmen, nōminis (*n*)	name
nōn	not
novus, -a, -um	new
nox, noctis (*f*)	night
numerus, -ī (*m*)	number
numquam	never
nunc	now

O

omnis, -is, -e	the whole, every, each
os, ossis (*n*)	bone

P

parō (1)	to prepare
pars, partis (*f*)	part
per (+ *acc.*)	through, along, over
pēs, pedis (*m*)	foot
petō, petere (3), **petīvī, petītum**	to seek, aim at, attack
pōnō, pōnere (3), **posuī, positum**	to put, place
porta, -ae (*f*)	gate
possum, posse (*irreg.*), **potuī**	to be able
postquam	after
(sē) praecipitāre	to hurl oneself, rush
praetereō, praeterīre (*irreg.*), **praeteriī, praeteritum**	to go past
prīmus, -a, -um	first
prope (+ *acc.*)	near
puella, -ae (*f*)	girl
puer, puerī (*m*)	boy

Q

-que	and
quem	whom
quī, quae, quod	who, which, that
quīdam, quaedam, quoddam	a certain, (plural) some
quod	because

R

redeō, redīre (*irreg.*), **rediī, reditum**	to return, go back
reprehendō, reprehendere (3), **reprehendī, reprehēnsum**	to blame, scold, reprimand
rīvus, -ī (*m*)	stream
rogō (1)	to ask
rūsticus, -a, -um	of or belonging to the country or farm

S

saepe	often
salūtō (1)	to greet
satis	enough
scelestus, -a, -um	wicked
sciō (4)	to know
scrībō, scrībere (3), **scrīpsī, scrīptum**	to write
sē	himself, herself, oneself, itself, themselves
sed	but
sedeō, sedēre (2), **sēdī, sessum**	to sit
semper	always
servus, -ī (*m*)	slave
sī	if
silentium, -ī (*n*)	silence
silva, -ae (*f*)	woods
sine (+ *abl.*)	without
sordidus, -a, -um	dirty
spectātor, spectātōris (*m*)	spectator, onlooker
spectō (1)	to watch, look at
stō, stāre (1), **stetī, statum**	to stand
sub (+ *abl.*)	under, beneath
subitō	suddenly
sum, esse (*irreg.*), **fuī**	to be
suprā (*adverb*)	above
suus, -a, -um	his, her, one's, its, their (own)

T

tamen	nevertheless
tandem	at last, at length
tantus, -a, -um	so great
tardus, -a, -um	slow
tē	you (singular; direct object)
templum, -ī (*n*)	temple

tempus, temporis (*n*)	time
eō tempore	at that time
teneō, tenēre (2), **tenuī, tentum**	to hold
tū	you (singular; subject)
tum	at that moment, then
tunica, -ae (*f*)	tunic
tuus, -a, -um	your (singular)

U

ubi	where, when
ūnus, -a, -um	one
urbs, urbis (*f*)	city

V

Valē! Valēte!	Goodbye!
veniō, venīre (4), **vēnī, ventum**	to come
videō, vidēre (2), **vīdī, vīsum**	to see
vīlicus, -ī (*m*)	overseer, farm manager
vīlla, -ae (*f*)	farmhouse
vīnea, -ae (*f*)	vineyard
vir, virī (*m*)	man
vīta, -ae (*f*)	life
volō, velle (*irreg.*), **voluī**	to wish, want, be willing